Fons of "Traditional Bamenda" and Partisan Politics in Contemporary Cameroon

Fons of "Traditional Bamenda" and Partisan Politics in Contemporary Cameroon

Reconstructing Identity and Cultural Meaning

Tatah Mbuy

SPEARS BOOKS
Denver, Colorado

Spears Books
An Imprint of Spears Media Press LLC
7830 W. Alameda Ave, Suite 103-247
Denver, CO 80226
United States of America

First Published in the United States of America in 2023 by Spears Books
www.spearsbooks.org
info@spearsmedia.com
Information on this title: www.spearsbooks.org/fons-of-traditional-bamenda

First published in Cameroon by Imprimrie de la CENC, Mvolyé, Yaounde, 2021

ISBN: 9781957296128 (Paperback)
ISBN: 9781957296135 (eBook)

Designed and typeset by Spears Media Press LLC
Cover designed by D. Kambem
Cover photo: 'Fons from Bamenda in Tiko Airport', December 1960, The National Archives UK

Distributed globally by African Books Collective (ABC)
www.africanbookscollective.com

DEDICATION

Prof. Bernard FONLON Shufai Ntoh Ndzev (1924-86). (*The Genuine Intellectual*): "The authority of the Fon is indisputable."

His Eminence Christian Cardinal TUMI (1930-2021). "The Fon incarnates the entire Ethnic Group. When he is relevant, he speaks with the authority of the Ancestors."

The Servant of God, Paul Mbiybe VERDZEKOV (1931-2010). "The culture of a people is the prism through which they see reality."

Fondly Remembered:
Prof. Michael ALETUM TABUWE
(1934-2020).
"There is a need to integrate our traditional political set up in the modern democratic overtures."

Prof. Daniel Noni LANTUM
Shufai woo Bastos, (1937-2021).
"The identity and quality of an African are found in his attachment to his cultural values."

Mgr Patrick Nyuydine LAFON
(The Priest-Philosopher with a cultural charm) 1952-2021.
"A people without a culture have no identity and cannot be respected."

Contents

List of Figures

FOREWORD

Prof. Verkijika G. Fanso

This is neither the first nor the last time that the attraction to, and the personal participation of some traditional rulers, in competitive politics has raised genuine concerns and the need for caution. Right from the colonial days with the Germans and the British, the Chiefs had to tread a very tight rope in the political arena. The *Southern Cameroons House of Chiefs* was a unique structure by the British who wanted to benefit from the power which the local traditional rulers already had over their population. These rulers gave advice to the administrators in traditional matters and also helped to resolve conflicts, collect taxes, and organize the people. In this way, they were of great assistance to the British administrators who quickly discovered that the chiefs had more control at the grassroots than anyone of them could have. There is no documented record anywhere of chiefs competing with their subjects for authority in Government. In the Bamenda Grassfields in particular, if any traditional ruler overstepped his bounds, the *Kwifon* (*Nwerong, Ngumba*) regulatory body in the palace brought him to order. This was because, the dignity, authority and sacredness of the Fon was such that no one contested it and it was never to be dragged into the mud by whoever.

Since the 1977 Chieftaincy Law, there have been major changes in the attitude of both the chiefs and the government. Chiefs were categorised and some created, to the extent that very few seem to understand the status, extent and limit of royal authority anymore. And this was not special to Cameroon! From the 8th to 12th August 2005, the *Pan African Association of Anthropologists* (PAAA) celebrated its 15th anniversary in Yaounde. One of the sticky issues discussed was the involvement of chiefs in partisan politics. Some of them had positioned themselves in multi-party politics, in a way that was at variance with the wishes and interests of their people (cf. Fokwang, 2009).[1]

Fr Tatah Mbuy has been inspired by the fact that since the re-introduction of multi-party politics in Cameroon in 1990, a good number of Chiefs, *Lamidos* and *Fons,* personally went into competitive politics with their subjects. The consequences have been disastrous as the society has been divided because members eye each other now from political viewpoints. This happened because some Fons and some administrators hardly understood the status of the traditional ruler in general and the Fon in particular. That is why Fr Tatah Mbuy, drawing from the experience in the North West Region of Cameroon, has done the duty of an anthropologist trying to point out first that the Fon is not an individual but an institution; and the individual who incarnates that institution does not just act as he wants. Secondly, the Fon in the Bamenda Grassfields is primarily a High Priest who liaises between the living and the "living-dead." He is the custodian of culture, the representative of the people and the epitome of neutrality and impartiality. Seen from this perspective, the Fon in Bamenda is a sacred institution which should be respected and not brought into partisan politics. Much as the individual who represents the institution of Fon is free to perform his duties as a citizen, one of the rights he must forfeit as Fon is to become overtly partisan, because that compromises his position of neutrality.

Those in Government who are trying to drag the Fons into becoming "auxiliaries of administration" in the sense in which we understand it today, need to reconsider the implications. It would be to the advantage of Government if the Fon were to remain the institution that it has always been. In this unique position, the Fon stands the chance of reconciling and bringing about peace in society. The armed conflict in Southern Cameroons (2016-2021) reached the ugly level it did, precisely because some of the Fons seemed to have forgotten their status and publicly declared support and membership for one political party over another.

Fr Tatah Mbuy raises alarm about what is happening and calls on the Fons to rethink the institutions they inherited, to act as true "fathers" to all people, and to become true custodians of culture.

1 Jude Fokwang, *Mediating Legitimacy: Chieftaincy and Democratisation in Two African Chiefdoms.* Langaa Research and Publishing, 2009.

ACKNOWLEDGMENTS

Every research work is a collective achievement as it engages so many resource persons that at the end, no individual can really take credit for it. I am therefore heartily grateful to the great number of men and women, scholars, politicians and administrators who showed interest in this work and made some suggestions. They all contributed directly or indirectly to its success. By the token of having engaged the quality and quantity of people that I did, this work should have no deliberate errors. But absolute perfection does not belong to our earthly existence; hence, every human endeavour stands to be corrected and improved upon. It was the saintly Oxford scholar, John Henry Cardinal Newman who made it clear to us that "*nothing would be done at all, if a man waited until he could do it so well that no one could find fault with it.*" We already make apologies for any errors that would be found and for any facts which may hurt. The intention was to make, not to mar!

This work benefited from the expertise of reputed historians notably Prof. Verkijika G. Fanso and Dr Willibroad Dze Ngwa. They read through the entire work and made great proposals. Mrs Fri Bime went through the research with the eyes of a literary scholar and made the language more viable. Mr Joseph Akombo combined his experience as DO, scholar and traditional adviser to a Fon, to give an insight which no other could have. I am profoundly grateful to the Fons of the North West and the Chiefs of the South West Regions who readily discussed their predicament with us. I considered it a bonus to have had some members of Government read through our script to ensure that we had both a balanced view and the right focus. This work had to be written at this time because it was the Servant of God, Paul Mbiybe Verdzekov who planted the guilt in me when he told me on several occasions: "A sin of omission is committed when we do nothing at the moment when something must be done." May God bless all of us!

Tatah Mbuy,
Yaounde, May 2021

INTRODUCTION

Figure A1. Some traditional rulers from the Bamenda Grassfields

In 1967, the Ministry of Primary Education and Social Welfare of West Cameroon published field research by two eminent Oxford scholars - Elizabeth Millicent Chilver and Phyllis Mary Kaberry. Their work was significantly entitled: *Traditional Bamenda: The Pre-colonial History and Ethnography of the Bamenda Grassfields.*[1] The stress on "traditional Bamenda" was purposeful because Chilver and Kaberry wrote about the history of a people for whom culture was, and has always been, a matter of life and death, flesh and blood, identity and sacredness. So, the people were intolerant towards anyone or any move meant to mess about with their culture.

1 E. M. Chilver and Phyllis M. Kaberry, *Traditional Bamenda: the pre-colonial history and ethnography of the Bamenda Grassfields,* National Government Publication, Buea, 1967.

Chilver and Kaberry knew from their personal experiences, for example, that the Fon in the Bamenda Grassfields was not just a person but a *unique institution* to be carefully studied and understood if one were to make any in-routes into cultural studies. And they spent time trying to understand the culture and setup of the people! In fact, they had no choice, because the Fons in the Bamenda Grassfields ruled well-organised and culturally knit states or Fondoms.

At this time the legendary Mbinkar Mbinglo (Sehm III) was ruling Nso' Fondom with unquestionable Divine rights, and no foreigner could just get into Nso'land and say or do as he wanted. The place of the Fon was always necessary for anything significant to happen. This was equally the time when Achirimbi II, the 10th Fon of Bafut could not be challenged by any of his subjects. The Fon had the final word in his entire Fondom, and nothing happened in Bafutland without Achirimbi being aware.

Chilver and Kaberry also quickly learned from their previous British countrymen and administrators that Foyn Ngam of Kom was "every inch a King" - a *lum nyam* (the greatest animal)[2]; so Komland was his unquestionable territory. It was at the same time when, even the Basel Missionaries, who came in for the lofty ambition of evangelization, would have told any foreigner that without the permission of Fon Galega II in Bali Nyonga, little or nothing could be achieved within Bali Fondom. Fon Angwafor III of Mankon, could tell the story in 2020, of what it meant to be Fon in "traditional Bamenda" of the 1960s and 70s.

The Fon was the main custodian of land and culture, primarily the traditional High Priest, the incarnation of the ethnic grouping and divine ancestral institution, not open to any manipulations, certainly not to partisan politics! Both the German and the British colonial masters to "traditional Bamenda" were quick to understand and respect this pivotal role of the Fon; the reason why the British in particular, recognized this power of royalty, and inspired by their "House of Lords," also established the "Southern Cameroons House of Chiefs" which lasted from 1961-1972.[3] The intention of the British was to seek the advice of traditional royal authority, while maintaining them as "the final indigenous decision-makers"[4] in their states.

By and large, the British colonial masters gained a lot from this inculturation

2 Cf. Report by Her Majesty's Government in the United Kingdom of Great Britain and Northern Ireland in the General Assembly of the United Nations on the Administration of Cameroons under United Kingdom Trusteeship for the year 1951, 23-24, (PRO).

3 Cf. Chem-Langhëe, Bongfen, *The Origins of the Southern Cameroons House of Chiefs*, The International Journal of African Historical Studies , Vol. 16, no.4, 1983, pp. 653-673.

4 *Ibid*, p. 653.

of Bamenda Grassfields culture; and it is within this background that we can appreciate and interpret the work of Chilver and Kaberry! Culture was sacrosanct and the Fon was, and could never have been suspected of any partiality or bias. He was truly "Father" to everyone, and his priority was clearly, the Common Good of his people! So, even in the forest regions of British Southern Cameroons where there were mostly "segmented societies" and chieftaincy "was at most very weakly developed," colonial authorities had to create customary chiefs because the authority of the Fon was at the centre of society.[5]

Today, a mighty lot has happened, bringing to light the perennial anthropological concern of "Cultures and Societies in a Changing World."[6] For every change there are always some "invariants" which everyone takes for granted will not change. This work was provoked by the fact that in our social change, many Fons in "traditional Bamenda" "positioned themselves in the multi-party era, sometimes at variance with the wishes or interests of their subjects,"[7] and conflict ensued!

The majority opinion of the subjects was that the Fon should remain neutral in partisan politics and should never publicly express or identify with one party over another.[8] But, the events leading up to, and during the armed conflict in the former "Southern Cameroons" indicate that it was due to their involvement in partisan politics with many of them taking sides with the ruling party that a good number of Fons had to escape from their Fondoms to remain alive. Some went into the diaspora as refugees, some lived elsewhere as "Internally Displaced Persons" (IDPs), and others were killed.

Such a situation constituted a *cultural sacrilege* which no normal person in "traditional Bamenda" could ever have thought of. Yet, despite this anomaly, there have been some arrangements, notably by the *evolués* and some politicians, to bring Fons more and more into partisan political life, and as "auxiliaries of administration." Curiously, although a good number of people today, including some Fons themselves, may not see the danger that looms in the horizons, anyone

5 Cf. Peter Geschiere, Chiefs and Colonial Rule in Cameroon: Inventing Chieftaincy, French and English Style, in *Africa: Journal of the International African Institute,* Vol. 63, No. 2 (1993), pp. 151-175.

6 Cf. Wendy Griswold, *Cultures and Societies in a Changing World,* 3rd Edition, Pine Forge Press, Los Angeles, 2008.

7 Jude Fokwang, *Mediating Legitimacy: Chieftaincy and Democratisation in Two African Chiefdoms,* Langaa Research & Publishing Centre, Mankon, Bamenda, 2009, p. v.

8 Cf. *Ibid,* p. 14.

who knows what the Fon means in "traditional Bamenda", will shudder to see the euphoria with which some Fons have been received into political parties.

Historians will tell us that it was precisely this excitement of Fons getting involved in partisan politics, that was largely responsible for a good amount of the atrocities associated with the armed conflict in Southern Cameroons from 2016 to 2021. Were these Fons aware of the consequence of their acts? Could they have acted otherwise? Brief, what can explain this change in attitude by some of the Fons, ministers, administrators and politicians? The fundamental "Principle of Causality" expressed in Aristotle's *Metaphysics,* states that whatever is moved is moved by another (*Quidquid movetur, ab alio movetur*!). Therefore, we must get to the root cause of this phenomenon if we truly want to fully understand it in its proper context.[9]

From 1960 to 1972, the Fons had a forum where they discussed, advised and interacted in Cameroon politics – the "House of Chiefs." The abolition of this "House" by Ahmadou Ahidjo in 1972, and the resurrection of a similar "House" in 2020 by Paul Biya, had diverse implications and complex consequences. But this work does not have the luxury to get into the details. However, we are forced to meditate on the fact that the Fon in "traditional Bamenda" is primarily, almost essentially, the ethnic *High Priest*. Therefore, his first and almost exclusive ministry is to intercede and mediate between the living and the "living-dead" of his Fondom. He is ***not an administrator*** in the sense in which we think about the profession today. In fact, the concept of Fon in "traditional Bamenda", CANNOT be taken out of a spiritual context. From the Catholic Church, we can make a limping analogy - just like the Catholic priest is called an administrator of the temporary goods of the Church, so in a similar sense, can the Fon in "traditional Bamenda" be called an "administrator."

If we try to make him an "auxiliary of administration," in the modern concept and application, we not only take him out of his real role, but we also tempt him without realising perhaps, to take an *a priori* stance for or against a cross-section of his own people. And this in itself, already brings an element of injustice and muffles the real status and significance of Fon. That is part of the sanity why for decades, the *Mbog Mbog* in Bassa country refused to be associated with, or recruited into the Cameroonian political administration, The Mbog Mbog always insisted that as the core traditional institution of authority, it is concerned with something more cultural, more spiritual, more sublime which gives profound meaning to the Bassa as a people. *Mutatis mutandis*, being a Fon in "traditional

9 Cf. Aristotle, *Posterior Analytics; APost.* 71 b 9–11. Cf. *APost.* 94 a 20.

Bamenda" is no trivial matter. The Fon is not, and should not be under the impulse of any political authority.

To demonstrate this cultural conviction, we shall divide our work into three parts, each subdivided into chapters. Since the Fon in "traditional Bamenda" is the locus of all cultural authority, we shall dedicate Part 1 of this work towards a general understanding of **The Traditional Ruler in Bamenda**, and the status of the Fon in particular. This is very important for those who are not from this area or for those who do not have the same set up to situate the Fon in his proper geopolitical context. Furthermore, this first part will give us the opportunity to explain that authority in "traditional Bamenda" is institutional and comes down from the Ancestors, hence it is divine, and that determines the manner in which the custodian relates and negotiates with others. The Fon is essentially a High Priest, a sacred institution with divine authority which is paramount and at the centre of relationships. When people have problems, it is to the Fon that they make their final recourse. So, the Fon is seen as the apex of neutrality and justice.

However, things and cultures change. In fact, culture is so dynamic that it is one of the greatest receptacles of change. And in the changing world of today, Africa in general, and Cameroon in particular, "seems to be in for profound political changes."[10] Hence Part 2 of this work will focus on **Partisan Politics in Contemporary Cameroon**. In two chapters, we give an overview of the evolution of party politics in Cameroon and how this affected the Fons. In multiparty politics in particular, the Fon had to negotiate his position very tactfully, especially as the people believe that their Fons should not get involved in what has so often been described as a "dirty game," "a game of interests." In this second part therefore, we show that despite social and cultural changes in society, the status of the Fon remains a non-variable in "traditional Bamenda." The Fon is a core-culture and a determinant of the cultural identity of the people.

But today we are dealing with an "android generation" for whom the culture of the people means very little. They are "digital natives" and most of them are such "cultural hybrids" that we need to reconstruct "cultural meaning" and identity for them. That is why Part 3 of our research is **A Search for Meaning**. In the modern world, the power game is played out in the virtual space of social media. Here, we construct reality, social problems and meaning. It is an era in which the media plays a central role in identification and interpretation of environmental issues.[11] Yet, if we must survive as a people and make genuine development,

10 Peter Geschiere, Chiefs and Colonial Rule in Cameroon, *Op.Cit.*, p. 151.

11 Cf. Manuel Castells, *Communication Power,* Oxford University Press, Oxford, 2009, pp.

we cannot become aliens to our roots, no matter how hybrid we have become.

The history and experience of sub-cultures today show us that there will never be a so called "global culture" or a "collective identity," because as the American communication theorist, James William Carey says it, all "technology is a totem for culture."[12] So, no matter how hybrid people become and how far away from their culture they grow, there is always an inner search for their roots. That is why we must heal the social problem which we have created with regards to the institution of Fonship in "traditional Bamenda." And we need to do this, not by seeking cosmetic solutions, but by getting to the roots. The perennial philosophy of the School men reminds us that when the "Cause finishes, the effect ceases" - *(Causa finita, effectus cessat)!* The root cause of all the confusion and painful armed conflict that rocked our society for over four years and more, lies in coming to terms with our understanding of culture; and in this dispensation, the proper understanding and respect for the Fon in "Traditional Bamenda," is key towards a meaningful and lasting solution to the social problems.

In this work, we constantly use the appellation "Bamenda Grassfields" (sometimes referred to as the *Western High Plateau*, or the *Western Highlands*) an expression we have borrowed from Chilver and Kabbery.

> In 1964 the Bamenda Grassfields, then composed of the three West Cameroon prefectures of Bamenda, Wum and Nkambe, had a population of almost 575,000, which was densest in the Bamenda prefecture, adjoining the populous Bamileke prefectures. By 1967 these three prefectures had been increased to five – Bamenda, Gwofon, Nso, Wum and Nkambe – by division of the former Bamenda prefecture into three (Bamenda, Gwofon and Nso) and the addition to Gwofon of the Widekum-Menka area formerly administered as part of Mamfe Division.[13]

The population of the Bamenda Grassfields is largely made of the Tikar and share a lot in common. They are very strict in adhering to their cultural identity and would spontaneously fight back any attempts by whosoever, to destroy their cultural values. In fact, people here are ready to die for what they believe

---

315-317.

12 James William Carey, Technology as a Totem for Culture. And a Defense of the Oral Tradition, in *American Journalism*, no.7, 1990, pp. 242-251.

13 Cf. Chilver and Kaberry, Chronology of the Bamenda Grassfields, in *Journal of African History*, Volume 11, Issue 2, April 1970, pp. 249–257.

in. They are so proud of their culture and identity that nothing will make them tread these realities away. Part of the reason for the armed conflict in the North West Region of Cameroon from 2016-2021, lies in the fact that the people are not easily intimidated, even by military might, into accepting what they are not convinced about. The Fon in this part of Cameroon is a divine institution; a moral body; a high priest whose authority is paramount and at the service of all subjects. The Fon cannot therefore be partisan in competitive politics, nor can the individual who incarnates that institution stand up at variance with the people; and this is the *status quaestionis* of this work!

PART 1

THE TRADITIONAL RULER IN BAMENDA

Figure A2. Fon Fobuzie Martin I of Chomba

"The Cameroon Chieftaincy Law contained in decree No. 77/245 of July 15, 1977 organizes traditional communities into chiefdoms."

"Chiefs are in principle chosen from families called upon to exercise traditional customary authority. The candidate to mount the throne must meet the physical and moral conditions required and must as far as possible know how to read and write."

This section of the work (Part 1) seeks to situate the institution of Fon within the general framework of traditional authority and rulership in the "Bamenda Grassfields." This part is divided into three chapters.

Chapter 1 considers **The Traditional Ruler as an Institution** not an event of an "individual." Each traditional ruler is installed to act as mediator between the people of the family and the "living dead." Hence, each ruler is sacred and his institution is divine. Each traditional ruler is never called by his proper name (except just before his burial) because he is both a corporate and moral person. That is why traditional rulership is seen as the locus of neutrality and justice, so, everyone expects fair treatment each time he is before a traditional ruler. In fact, all traditional rulers are expected to be the custodians of the cultural heritage which has been handed down from generations.

This is the context from which Chapter 2 emerges; it presents and examines **The Divine Authority of the Fon**. The Fon is the apex of traditional authority and represents the bond among the people, and between the people and their "gods." The choice of a Fon is essentially the business of the ancestors who are consulted by a very special group of elders (the "Fon-Makers"). The Fon is the chief High Priest of the ethnic group, the paramount ruler of the people, the titular owner of the land, and the one who is specially chosen by the ancestors to have husbandry over the cultural heritage of the land.

That is why, Chapter 3 considers **The Fon at the Heart of Public Relations**. He rules with Divine authority and relates with the people from that perspective. He is not an "administrator" in the profane and conventional understanding of the word. Therefore, at all times, he acts for and on behalf of his people, seeking neither self-interest nor private gain.

Chapter 1

THE TRADITIONAL RULER AS AN INSTITUTION

Figure 1.1. Some Traditional Rulers of Aghem, Wum

In order to understand the significance of the Fon in traditional Bamenda, we have to situate "him" within the cultural context and understanding of any "traditional ruler" in local geopolitics; and the implications here go far beyond the Cameroonian French translation and construction of *autorité traditionnelle* (traditional authority, or ruler). As two eminent Nigerian scholars rightly point out:

The place of traditional rulers in contemporary society is a knotty one in practically all of the Third World. Supposedly caught between modernism and traditionalism, few of these societies have been able to provide more than makeshift solutions to the problem....

There is clearly an insufficient understanding of both the dynamics of

> institutionalized traditional rulership and of the different factors, historical and environmental, which interact with it. (Hence) too often, the fate and future of traditional rulership, which is indeed, a central problem for post-colonial policy makers, is treated as a matter of trial and error.[1]

A Cameroonian political scientist and senior lecturer, Cosmas Cheka considered similar issues and concluded that traditional authority in contemporary Cameroon is at the crossroads, largely due to the misunderstanding of the real concept, role and meaning of traditional rulership in the Bamenda Grassfields in particular.[2]

This chapter therefore sets out to explain who and what a traditional ruler is in traditional Bamenda; it briefly examines the different categories of traditional rulers and presents their basic mission as custodians of culture, moral persons, and the incarnation of the people. The aim here is to throw more light on the fact that the traditional ruler in Bamenda is neither an ***administrator*** in the sense in which modern politics understands it, nor should he be made into one. To appreciate the difficulty in trying to rethink "traditional authority" in categories of modern Cameroon politics, there is a need for a critical conceptual and analytical examination of the modern and the traditional ruler in Cameroon in general, and in the Bamenda Grassfields in particular.

And the key to this examination, is to understand the word "tradition" used here with all the force from its original Latin verb – *tradere* – to transmit, to handover and to give for the sake of safeguarding. As used in this chapter, we understand "tradition" to include all the "beliefs, objects or customs performed or believed in the past, originating in it, transmitted through time by being taught by one generation to the next, and are performed or believed in the present."[3]

Three important realities underlie human existence in traditional Bamenda: ***identity***, the ***community*** and ***cultural values.*** These elements are so interrelated that one cannot be separated from the other because, the identity of a person is best understood in the context of his community relationships and his adherence to culture. The people of Bamenda believe that the "soul" is the life-principle

1 O. M. Laleye and Victor Ayeni, "On the Politics of Traditional Rulership," *International Journal of Politics, Culture, and Society*, Vol. 6, No. 4 (Summer, 1993), p. 555.

2 Cf. Cosmas Cheka, "Traditional Authority at the Crossroads of Governance in Republican Cameroon." *Africa Development / Afrique Et Dévelopement*, vol. 33, no. 2, 2008, pp. 67–89.

3 Thomas A. Green, Folklore: An Encyclopedia of Beliefs, Customs, Tales, Music, and Art. ABC-CLIO, California, 1997, p. 80.

which gives sacredness to a human being; it is the seat of moral behaviour and the locus for interpersonal relationship. Every person therefore has something divine in him and that is what makes for his dignity and sacredness as a person. Hence as the people of Nso', one of the biggest ethnic groups in traditional Bamenda, put it: a person is his soul (*wir dze kiyoy*) but this *kiyoy* has meaning only in as much as it also enables the individual to perform morally good acts; and morally good acts are part of character. Here, a person is defined by his character (*wir dze lii*); and an essential element of character is the manner in which a person relates to others. Hence the Nso' people often say: "a person is a person because of another" *(wir dze wir bi' wir)*.[4]

So, no matter how much a person owns and whatever position he occupies, if such a person does not relate well with others, he is considered as a "nobody" (*wir kisang*). These are the central elements to understand when thinking of a ruler in the true sense of a typical Bamenda person.

A traditional ruler is first and foremost, a person in the sense above, because an integral part of his mission is to ensure and safeguard the sacredness and dignity of the human being; and as the ancient Romans believed: "*nemo dat quod non habet*" (one cannot give what he has not got). The identity of each person, including that of the traditional ruler, gets its proper meaning from the manner in which he integrates in the community and his adherence to culture, understood here as the standard of morality. Note has to be taken that the "community" is of paramount importance to traditional Bamenda; the reason why the people believe very strongly in the *Ubuntu* philosophy and logic: "I am because we are; and because we are, therefore I am."[5]

Every traditional ruler is chosen on the basis that he will do everything to ensure this community spirit of *ubuntu*. So, a ruler is chosen first and foremost as the one who holds the community together; and the community here, consists of the living and the dead. Hence, a traditional ruler is essentially a liaison between the living and the dead. His *primary duty is to keep the community united by pouring libation*, or if need be, *by offering sacrifices on behalf of the living*. This means that in traditional Bamenda, every traditional ruler is first and foremost, a *High Priest* of the community, composed of the living and the dead, and the dead are not really dead but are to be regarded rather as the *living-dead*.

4 Cf. Tatah Mbuy, *The Nso' Concept of Man*, Philosophical Dissertation, Unpublished, Bambui, 1979.

5 Cf. Ramose, Mogobe B. "The philosophy of ubuntu and ubuntu as a philosophy" in P. H. Coetzee & A. P. J. Roux (eds.), *The African philosophy Reader*, 2nd ed., Routledge. London, 2003, pp. 230–238.

> "The relationship between those living on earth and the ancestors is very close, since the living owe their existence to the ancestors from whom they receive everything necessary for life. On the other hand, the living-dead can 'enjoy' their ancestorship only through the living clan community. In this way, a kind of interaction - hierarchically organized from top to bottom and vice versa – is created."[6]

It was the Kenyan anthropologist, John Samuel Mbiti who coined the term "living-dead" to portray the African belief that when a person physically dies on this earth, he lives on as a spirit in the sublime world of the ancestors and God.[7] In this way, the living-dead gain a new existence - partly "human" but largely "spiritual." This new status makes the *living-dead* more powerful and more able to influence those who are still physically alive. Hence, it is believed that the identity and survival of any community depend very much on how well their traditional ruler is able to keep the living and the living-dead in harmony with each other. And that is the reason why the traditional ruler (even when he is chosen as a unique individual,) is never considered as a *monad*[8] with no true casual relation with others; instead, he is profoundly seen as an institution by itself.

a) The Traditional Ruler as a Divine Institution

An *institution* is an established structure devoted to the promotion of a particular cause or program.

Institutions are brought into being by culture and collective choice; they have roles and expectations for and from the society. Institutions arise, develop and function in a pattern of social self-organization beyond conscious intentions of the individuals involved.[9] Concretely, this means that an institution is a structure set up to govern both social and individual behaviour in a community, but it is independent of individual wishes and interests, even when that individual is in charge of it. Brief, an institution is a social body or entity with its own clear identity as a juridical, moral person. This is the sense in which we are to understand the concept of "*Traditional Ruler as an Institution*" in traditional Bamenda.

6 Bénézet Bujo, *The Ethical Dimension of Community. The African Model and the Dialogue between North and South,* Pauline Publications, Africa, Nairobi, 1997, pp. 15-16.

7 Cf. John S. Mbiti, *African Religions and Philosophy,* Heinemann, London, 1969.

8 Cf. Gottfried Wilhelm Leibniz, in *Monadologia* (1714).

9 Cf. "Institution" in Godfrey M. Hodgson, *Journal of Institutional Economics*, 11 March 2015, 497–505.

In Bamenda, leadership is seen as a sacred "ancestral institution" and heritage which has come down from the founding ancestors through one generation to another. Hence it is divine, even if it is established with all the appearances of a human structure. The ruler who is chosen is a human being. But from the moment he assumes authority, he is seen as a sacred person with dignity. That is why only the best person is usually discretely groomed and chosen as successor by the reigning ruler long before he dies. So, "traditional authority" is not a *post for competition or election in the contemporary sense of the word.* In traditional Bamenda, rulers are not "elected" by the majority or chosen by public administration. Traditional rulership is achieved by inheritance, following a well-defined ritual, which may differ in detail from one group to the other, but the aim is to ensure that the best of the heirs, is chosen. That is why, once an heir has been chosen and brought by the regulatory traditional society (*kwifoyn* or *nwerong*), it is difficult for the individual in question to reject the choice.

Once the individual accepts the throne, he is aware that from that moment, he represents, not just himself and his competencies, but is seen and respected as an institution. The traditional ruler in Bamenda is always seen primarily as a liaison with the ancestors; and he is therefore sacred and divine. The individual who occupies the position of a traditional ruler, loses his personal identity as it were, and assumes the important sacred role which he now incarnates. That is why in many societies, he neither greets people with his hands, nor is his personal name ever called again (except when he physically dies). Otherwise, he is seen and spoken of as a moral body, as a custodian of culture, as a representative of the people, and as the link between the living and the ancestors. He is more of a divine institution than the individual we knew before his assumption of traditional rulership. As in Ghana, "the institution of Chieftaincy is (primarily seen as) the link between the past and the future."[10]

b) Categories of Traditional Rulers

For a good number of people who are not well versed in the cultural organization of traditional Bamenda, one traditional ruler (what the French call *autorité traditionnel* or *Chefs)* can just be substituted by another as head of a group. But traditional rulers in Bamenda are in different categories and have diverse portfolios ranging from *Family Heads, Clan* and *Lineage Lords* to the unique "tribal" authority - the Fon - who encapsulates all traditional authority.

10 Monika Różalska. "Between Tradition and Modernity: The Role of Chiefs in the National Development and Local Governance in Ghana," *Politeja*, no. 42 (2016), p. 381.

i) Family Heads: Benezet Bujo tells us that: "The African person lives within an extended family."[11] Monde Makiwane and Chammah Kaunda describe what this means:

> Family in the African context often refers to what in western terms would be the extended family. A family is generally constituted by three processes, which are blood relations, sexual unions and adoption. Societally sanctioned sexual unions between (two and in cases of polygamists, which are not uncommon in Africa, more than two) adults of opposite sexes, and on the other hand, blood relations in Africa typically constitute wider relationship than those that are characteristically in Western nuclear families. African families are typically extended to include aunts, uncles, grandparents, cousins and other relatives that form a family that functions in unison. The broad concept of family in many African societies is illustrated in Mandela's autobiography *Long Walk to Freedom* where he states, 'My mother presided over three huts at Qunu, which as I remember, were always filled with babies and children of my relations. In fact, I hardly recall any occasion as a child when I was alone. In African culture, the sons and daughters of one's aunts and uncles are considered as brothers and sisters, not cousins.' In several African communities, family is not limited to space and time, thus, it cuts across generations, relatives living far and near, the living and those who have joined the ancestors, as well as the ancestors themselves who continue to play a role in the lives of the living.[12]

In many African societies, the words for aunt, uncle, nephew, niece, and cousin, do not exist. We simply have father, mother, brother and sister; hence one person could have more than one, and possibly four, five or more mothers, fathers, brothers and sisters at a time. These express the intimacy and relationship created by kinship.

ii) Different Titles for Various Family Heads: In traditional Bamenda, families have historic, numeric and cultural significance. The more significant any family is in any of these regards, the more importance it is given in society, and

11 Benezet Bujo, The Ethical Dimension of Community, *Op.Cit,* p. 15.

12 Monde Makiwane and Chammah J. Kaunda, *Families and Inclusive Societies in Africa,* https://www.un.org/development/desa/family/wp-content/uploads/sites/23/2018/05/1-2.pdf, Retrieved Monday, 4 January 2021.

the more important is their ruler.

The Nso' Fondom, for example, comprises of four categories. The first of these are that of *Won-Nto',* the exogamous royal descent group made up of the descendants of any Fon of Nso' to the fourth generation through agnatic lines and to the third through uterine connections. At the fifth generation in the male line and fourth in the female, the progeny rank as *Duy* (cadet royals), and these form the second social category in Nso'. The third social category is that of the *M'taar* the members of free commoner patriclans, who represent themselves as inhabitants of the land in which the ruling dynasty later established itself. They refer to themselves as the original owners of Nso'land who freely offered allegiance to the first rulers of Nso' in return for special privileges. The fourth social category is that of the *Nsheelav* or *Nshiy se lav* retainers or palace attendants, whose male members have a duty to palace service and are in charge of the welfare of the royal house.[13]

Each of these four social categories, play a very crucial role essential to the life of Nso'. The *Won-Nto'* provide the ruling dynasty; the *Duy* provide the Seven State Councillors (*Vibay ve Saamba)* or first rank advisers of the Fon. The *M'taar* provide the mother of the Fon (*Yee Fon*) and the *M'tar* lineage heads protect the Fon mystically and call him to order for any misconduct. Finally, the *Nsheelav* category provide the *attaanto'* or court officials and messengers of the Fon. Also worth noting is the fact that each family in Nso' identifies itself with one of these four categories at various levels – as a *little grouping of family members*; as a *big influential family* or *sub-lineage*; as a *bigger influential family* or *lineage;* as a *sub-clan of few lineages*; as *a clan;* and as an *ethnic group* made of *clans.* At each of these levels, the family head is given a special title of "rulership," with the title of Fon given exclusively to the paramount ruler of the ethnic group.

iii) Government Categorization of Traditional Rulers: Problems of Nomenclature: Decree No. 77/245 of 25 July 1977 on the organization of traditional chieftaincies in Cameroon groups all traditional rulers together, refers to them as "chiefs" (*Chefs)* and classifies them into First, Second, and Third Class Chiefs. Even the anthropologist Prof. Paul Nchoji Nkwi, follows this appellation but states that all "chiefs" who had a high degree of prestige, social integration, and large area of influence were ranked as "Grade One Chiefs." Only the Fons of Kom, Nso, Bafut, and Bali Nyonga qualified for this first place (and of recent,

13 Cf. Bongfen Chem-Langhëe, and Verkijika G. Fanso, "Social Categories, Local Politics and the Uses of Oral Tradition in Nso', Cameroon," *Paideuma,* 43, 1997, p. 315.

the Fon of Mankon).[14]

The 1977 decree states that a *First Class Chief* must have at least two second Class Chiefs under his jurisdiction. According to Nkwi, the criteria for second class chiefs "was the personality of the incumbent plus his prestige."[15] In fact, according to the Government classification, all the other chiefs in the North West Region outside the first class are *Second Class*. In the same classification, the government accords to all village heads, (or heads of communities in urban areas), the title of *Third Class Chiefs*.[16]

It is important to note here that the classification by Government contained in this decree, does not take cognizance or show sensitivity to the traditional implications and heavy weight of the title of Fon in traditional Bamenda. In fact, the decree seems to put the Fon in the North West on the same level as a "Chief" in the Southwest. Yet as the Dutch anthropologist, Peter Geschiere, rightly points out, in the South West, "prior to colonial conquest, Chieftaincy was at most very weakly developed."[17] In traditional Bamenda on the contrary, there were always categories of traditional rulers and chiefs with the Fon as paramount. In fact, you cannot have more than one Fon at the same time in the same area of jurisdiction. But there can be many traditional rulers in their different ranks, in the same area. The paramountcy and supremacy of the Fon in traditional Bamenda is culturally uncontested. However, whether a traditional ruler in question is a Clan head, a Chief or a Fon, each is considered as a ***Corporate*** and ***Moral Person***.

c) The Traditional Ruler as a Corporate and Moral Person

A *Corporate Person* is a legal entity or association which involves more than one *person* but which has met the legal requirements to operate as a single *person*. Lucy Philip Mair, the British anthropologist subscribes that in most of Africa, the traditional ruler is much more than the individual who fulfils a function. Rather, he is "a symbol, a rallying point," an incarnation of the people and a representation of all the ancestral and cultural values of the people. In fact, he can rightly be called a corporate person.[18] That is the reason why in many societies,

14 Paul Nchoji Nkwi, "Cameroon Grassfield Chiefs and Modern Politics," in *Paideuma* 25 (1979), pp. 99-100.

15 Paul Nchoji Nkwi, Ibid, p. 100.

16 Cf. Traditional Rulers, in http://www.northwest-cameroon.com/home-86-inner-0.html, retrieved 4 January 2021

17 Peter Geschiere, "Chiefs and Colonial Rule in Cameroon: Inventing Chieftaincy, French and British Style." *Africa: Journal of the International African Institute*, vol. 63, no. 2, 1993, p. 152.

18 Cf. Lucy Philip Mair, "African Chiefs Today. The Lugard Memorial Lecture for 1958." *Africa:*

the traditional ruler neither shakes hands with others, nor is his personal name ever called in public. Since he is the incarnation of the people, it is believed that he does not "die." In traditional Bamenda, a euphemism is used to announce the death of a ruler, especially the Fon. He is said to be "missing" or that the "sun has set" on the people.

Traditionally, all the subjects work for the good of the ruler; the people work his farm, bring all the strange game from their hunting to the ruler and go to him to seek solutions about any conflict or difficulty. They believe that the traditional ruler is endowed with extraordinary wisdom (*sem vifoni* in Nso') induced into him by the ancestors. That is why the traditional ruler is always credited with a high moral sense, dignity and a well-formed conscience. He is a *moral person*!

The idea of a *moral person* is so deeply a part of every person's social life that philosophers and social theorists have an obligation to determine what constitutes the idea of a moral person in the population at large.

A moral person is primarily a virtuous person who is restricted by the difference between what is good and what is bad; what is right and what is wrong. A virtuous person does not dangle between truth and falsehood, between justice and injustice. He knows what to do and when to do it. A *moral person* has a well-formed conscience and obeys it in every decision; in fact, he is a symbol of objectivity, fairness and justice.[19]

In traditional Bamenda, the ruler is expected to be a person of very high moral standard; that is the reason why the people put all their trust in him and take whatever he says for the truth. No one expects the traditional ruler to be corrupt, to tell lies and to manipulate his own people. So, his word was always taken as final. It is in this light that the compound of the traditional ruler in general, and the palace of the Fon in particular, was always seen as neutral ground where any person could find refuge. When subjects have their difficulties and conflicts, they spontaneously bring them to the traditional ruler because they believe in his deep sense of justice, sanctioned by the ancestors.

d) The Traditional Ruler as the Locus of Neutrality and Justice

Neutrality is the tendency not to take *sides* or get involved in a conflict. In colloquial use, *neutral* can be synonymous with *unbiased, impartial,* and *objective.* However, being neutral does not mean that one may not have a side or is not a

---

Journal of the International African Institute, vol. 28, no. 3, 1958, pp. 194-199.

19 Cf. Paul A. Wagner, "The Idea of a Moral Person." *Journal of Thought*, vol. 18, no. 2, 1983, pp. 85–88.

side itself. That is why the Associated Students of Madison strongly believed and stated that, "Neutrality is distinct (though not exclusive) from apathy, ignorance, indifference, double-think, equality, agreement, and objectivity."

Apathy and indifference each imply a level of carelessness about a subject, though a person exhibiting neutrality may feel bias on a subject but choose not to act on it. A neutral person can also be well-informed on a subject and therefore need not be ignorant.

Since they can be biased, a neutral person need not feature double-think (i.e., accepting both sides as correct), equality (i.e., viewing both sides as equal), or agreement (a form of group decision-making. Here it would require negotiating a solution on everyone's opinion, including one's own which may not be unbiased). "Objectivity suggests siding with the more reasonable position, where reasonableness is judged by some common basis between the sides, such as logic. Neutrality implies tolerance regardless of how disagreeable, deplorable, or unusual a perspective might be."[20]

In moderation and mediation, neutrality is often expected to make judgments or facilitate dialogue independent of any bias, putting emphasis on the process rather than the outcome. For example, a neutral party is seen as a party with no conflict of interest and is expected to operate as if it has no bias. Neutral parties are often perceived as more trustworthy, reliable, and safe. This is the idea of neutrality that the people of Bamenda expect to find in all their traditional rulers. They have always desired and gotten this off them, because neutrality is the only guarantee for justice.

Justice is the virtue by which we give to each person what he deserves. It is founded on the fact that each and every human person is created in the Image and Likeness of God, and therefore share an equality in dignity as persons. So, there is no human being who is more "human" than others; no one who is more of a "person" than other persons.

It is on this basis that justice or fair-play is built; everyone should be given the right to play on a level ground with the same rules and conditions. This is what is often known as ***Social Justice***. However, each of us can only contribute and receive according to one's capacity and talent. Hence, we talk of ***Distributive Justice*** – giving to each person according to his capacity. Outcomes should be based upon inputs. Therefore, an individual who has invested a large amount should justly receive more from the group than someone who has contributed

20 Cf. *"Associated Students of Madison, Viewpoint Neutrality in Funding Decisions."* *Wisc.edu*. Retrieved 4 January 2021.

very little. Justice also demands that the rules must be impartially followed and consistently applied in order to generate an unbiased decision. No one is above the law, hence we talk about ***Procedural*** or ***Legal Justice***. People also deserve to make amends and restore the damage they have caused others by their words or deed. That is why we also talk about ***Restorative Justice***. Finally, it is important to be just and to practice justice so as to deter those who are tempted to commit crimes or trample on the rights of others. Thus, justice can also become a deterrent or what is called ***Retributive Justice***. Whatever type of justice it may be, justice must become the norm and be implemented; and this is what the people of traditional Bamenda have always expected of their traditional rulers.

e) The Traditional Ruler as Custodian of Cultural Legacy

The American sociologist, Wendy Griswold observes that "culture is one of those words that people use all the time but have trouble in defining."[21]

Nonetheless, the English scholar, Sir Edward Burnett Tylor has given us a working description stating that "culture...is that complex whole which includes knowledge, belief, art, morals, law, custom, and any other capabilities and habits acquired by man as a member of a society."[22] In brief, Tylor sees culture as a *complex whole,* an omnibus concept which involves all significant human acts.

There are no people without a culture; and culture does not just happen. According to the American anthropologist, Clifford Geertz, culture "denotes an historically transmitted pattern of meanings embodied in symbols, a system of inherited conceptions expressed in symbolic forms by means of which men communicate, perpetuate and develop their knowledge about and attitudes towards life."[23] That is why it is often agreed that culture defines the identity of a people. So, in order to keep a people together, to give them a sense of meaning, it is crucial to keep their culture. And this is what the people of traditional Bamenda expect of their traditional rulers. Culture links the people with their ancestors, and since traditional rulers are the liaison between the living and their ancestors, one of the main duties of the ruler is to be the custodian of the cultural legacy of the people.

A ***cultural legacy*** is the inheritance of ***cultural*** traits that influence our success or failure. They are often determined by cultural practices that have been passed

21 Wendy Grisword, *Cultures and societies in a changing world*, Pine Forge, Los Angeles, 2008, p. 1.

22 Edward B. Tylor, *Primitive culture,* vol. 1, Gordon Press, New York, 1976, p. 1.

23 Clifford Geertz, *The Interpretation of Cultures,* Basic Books, New York, 1973, p. 1.

down through each generation from centuries ago. *The cultures of our ancestors (even the aspects we no longer practice or ascribe to) influence our present-day behaviours.* Cultural Legacy implies a shared bond, our belonging to a community.

It represents our history and our identity, our bond to the past, to our present, and the future. Cultural legacy is a heritage which often brings to mind artifacts (paintings, drawings, prints, mosaics, sculptures), historical monuments and buildings, as well as archaeological sites. But the concept of cultural legacy is even wider than that, and has gradually grown to include all evidence of human creativity and expression: photographs, documents, books and manuscripts, and instruments, etc., either as individual objects or as collections. Today, towns, underwater heritage, and the natural environment are also considered part of cultural heritage since communities identify themselves with the natural landscape. All peoples make their contribution to the culture of the world. That is why it is important to respect and safeguard all cultural heritage. Traditional rulers in Bamenda are expected to guard the cultural legacies of the people. In fact, they are seen as the custodians of these legacies, and should at no time, and for whatever reason, trade them away, or worse, destroy them.

We have indicated so far that in traditional Bamenda, there are a number of basic issues and concerns which the people expect from every traditional ruler, beginning from the smallest to the highest. When it comes to the *Fon*, who sums up in himself all the expectations that the people have of each and all traditional rulers, there can be no compromise. And that is why it is important that in our next chapter we explain, within context, the significance of Fon as a unique and Divine Authority; a traditional High Priest of the people.

Chapter 2

THE DIVINE STATUS AND AUTHORITY OF THE FON

Figure 2.1. HRH Fon Moolo of Nkar, Bui Division

The concept of the sacredness or divinity of a king originated in prehistoric times when the ruler was usually seen as an incarnation, a manifestation or an agent of the supernatural. In fact, in some of the ancient kingdoms, the ruler was regarded as a god or identified with some god. For example, in ancient Egypt, the *Pharoah* was identified with the *Sky god* or the *Horus,* or with the *Sun god* – the *Re, Amon*, or the *Aton.*[1]

A similar belief existed in traditional Bamenda about the divine status of the Fon. He is the highest instance of traditional authority and rulership and

1 Cf. Claus Westermann, "Sacred Kingship," *Encyclopedia Britannica,* 15th Edition, 1974.

he exercises power which extends to every sphere of human life - physical or metaphysical, profane or spiritual. In fact, the Fon is enthroned primarily to ensure and sustain the bond between the living and the living-dead. So, his enthronement, always includes some days of seclusion when the Fon is said to commune with, and receives wisdom from the ancestors and the gods. He is therefore considered as a living link with the ancestors, the reason why his status is thought of as divine.

a) The Divine Status of the Fon

Five essential elements mark the Fon out as a divine and unique personality. First and foremost, as we indicated already, the Fon is the bond and liaison between the living and the living-dead; so he is primarily the chief ***High Priest***, and this is the sole reason for which he is installed Fon. Second, he is the *incarnation of his people* (living and dead) and therefore the paramount ruler and owner of the land. Nothing of serious import can happen in his land without his permission. Third, the choice and enthronement of each Fon follows a well-known ***spiritual ritual***, performed by special *Fon-Makers* or elders, and ratified by the ancestors so as to give the Fon divine status and authority. Fourth, the Fon is the *custodian of culture and the land* - all the heritage and legacies of the ethnic group. So, he is under moral obligation never to trade off any of these, for whatever reason or gain. Finally, the Fon is a *social symbol of neutrality, justice* and the *Common Good.*

Each of these elements, fully understood singly, but always present in coordination with the others, makes the Fon different from any other person in his social grouping. Let us briefly explain each of these five elements which give the Fon the special divine status which he is believed to possess.

1) The Fon as Liaison Between the Living and the Dead

In traditional Bamenda, rulership is hereditary and primarily meant to be the bond and liaison between and among people of the same society. As Francis Njoku rightly puts it, for many Africans, life is a communal affair which involves a relationship and communion between man, God, ancestors, divinities, other men and the land.[2] And in traditional Bamenda, the Fon has the unique mission to ensure and guarantee that this relationship remains healthy and cordial. That is why every traditional ruler in Bamenda is seen and understood as the "high priest" of the family or group. The Fon, in particular, is clearly instituted

2 Cf. Francis Njoku, *Essays in African Philosophy, Thought and Theology.* Clacom, Owerri, 2002.

to ensure the desired unity and solidarity among family members and among all who belong to the clan or ethnic group – alive or dead.

The Fon is that bond which keeps all the people together and lubricates the liaison between those who are living and those who have travelled to the world of the ancestors. The dead are not cut off from the living, for they may reveal themselves in dreams or appear to their living relations to give instructions, warnings or information. They may summon living relatives to appear before them to explain their misconduct, and may punish them.[3]

Since life in Africa involves both those who are still physically alive and those who have "travelled the journey beyond,"[4] the Fon is established as the institution which keeps the bond between the two intact.

A *bond* is a relationship between people or groups based on shared beliefs, feelings, interests, or experiences; it suggests something or someone who keeps two or more people together and brings about mutual trust and friendship among them. People who are bonded together care about each other, they are in deep solidarity and are answerable to one authority. According to the American sociologist, Travis Hirschi, "elements of social bonding include attachment to families, commitment to social norms and institutions, involvement in activities, and the belief that these things are important."[5] At a religious level, the phrase "bonds of faith," describes the spiritual and religious ties or agreements that form religious communities, and points to the essential and existential meaning expressed in its Latin root, *religare*, "to bind."

In Latin, a "bond" denotes that which unites individuals, people, communities, and nations to each other via the ultimate reality, be it God, *Allah*, or another sacred symbol.[6] And it is with this meaning and implication of "bond" that we speak of the Fon as the ***bond*** that keeps the society together in traditional Bamenda.

Without the Fon there are no people, and without the people there is no Fon. One gives meaning and identity to the other. That is why the Fon is not

3 Cf. Kofi Asare Opuku, *West African Traditional Religion*. F. E. P., Lagos, 1978, p. 137.

4 Offiong Offiong Asuquo, "A rationalization of an African concept of life, death and the hereafter," in *American Journal of Social and Management Sciences*, Science Huβ, http://www.scihub.org/AJSMS, 2011.

5 Travis Hirschi, "Social Bond Theory," *Causes of Delinquency*, University of California Press, Berkeley, 1969, p. 16.

6 Cf. Jacob K. Olupuna, "Bonds, Boundaries, and Bondage of Faith" in *Harvard Divinity Bulletin*, 41, 2, 2013.

just a person, he is a BOND which keeps together the society - the living and the living dead. Therefore, although an individual is enthroned to assume this serious mission, the very fact of being the uniting factor, gives him both a moral and spiritual obligation to live up to expectation. And that is why the Fon communes with the ancestors to acquire from them the moral rectitude and divine power to keep the people together. He is the incarnation of the people taken together.

2) The Fon as the Incarnation of the People

The word "incarnation" literally means "taking on flesh." It is mostly used in the religious sphere, particularly in Christianity where Jesus of Nazareth is believed to be the embodiment of God-made-Man. By extension, the word is usually used in other disciplines to signify a sentient being who is the material manifestation of an entity, or a deity. When we say that the Fon is an incarnation of the People, we intend to express the belief that the Fon is an individual manifestation of the entire society. Hence, in traditional Bamenda, when he is still alive, the Fon is never referred to by his personal name or identification. He is always spoken of in the majestic plural: "*They*," and relatively very few speak directly to him; most speak through a mediator, even if all are speaking the same language.

In Christianity, the *Incarnation,* is a dogma, a teaching that in Christ Jesus we encounter the Supreme expression of the Godhead, and the extraordinary locus where God and Man meet. Hence Jesus is truly God and truly Man.

In a similar manner, for the people of traditional Bamenda, the Fon is incarnated in the people and the people in the Fon. That is why all the people are referred to, in Nso', as "*wir fon*" (the Fon's People). So, anything done to the Fon is considered as having been done to the people and vice versa. Without the people the Fon has no meaning and identity, just like without the Fon, the people are dispersed and lose an essential element of their identity. The relationship between the Fon and the people is so symbiotic that one cannot and will not exist without the other. And since the people are a creation of God, the Fon, as their leader, has divine status and his enthronement follows a well laid out spiritual ritual.

3) The Sacred Enthronement Ritual for a Fon

Fonship in traditional Bamenda is always ritualised; in fact, we can say that it is the ritual of enthronement which "makes the Fon." A ritual is a religious or solemn ceremony consisting of a series of actions performed according to a prescribed order. In Bamenda, there are very specific rituals to choose, enthrone and present the new Fon to the people. And each of these rituals is meant to make the institution of Fon more visible and to effect the induction of the individual into his office. In fact, in the ritual of investiture, the Fonship as it were, "seizes" the Fon. So, far from being passive or even imaginary reflexes of the social order, the rituals for the enthronement and presentation of the Fon are sacred instruments and approaches which maintain and convince participants of the reality of royal powers. Most of these rituals take place among, and by a select group of elders. And after these ritual processes which culminate with communion with the Ancestors, the new Fon feels changed in his person.

From then onward, the Fon takes responsibility and is consulted for ensuing events (a fall of rain, mysterious deaths) which affect the people.[7] These sacred rituals for enthronement may differ in detail from place to place, but common to all, is the fact that they are the prerogative of a council of elders or *Fon-makers*. There is no written manual to which these elders make reference, but each knows exactly what is to be done. The incantations follow an agreed pattern which expresses the real desire of the people to have a Fon who will link the people with their ancestors and the world of the spirits. An essential part of the ritual is the moment when the new Fon communes with his ancestors in order to gain wisdom (in Nso' this is called *Sem Vifoni*, or the wisdom of the rulers). During this moment, the new Fon is kept alone for almost seven days in the ancestral hut, and all food is secretly brought to him. According to the belief of the people, it is during this time that the Fon is shown how to transform into other animals for the sake of moving around easily in his Fondom; and also, for the sake of gaining the ability to fight witches and wizards in his Fondom. He is equally given the task of being the main custodian of the culture of the people.

4) The Fon as Main Custodian of Culture

If we want to know and understand a people, the best way is to study their culture since this is their identification mark as a group. Yet culture is such a troublesome concept to define, because, "there is not a single, eternal definition"[8] of it.

In fact, according to Gottfried O. Lang, "it is difficult to encompass in a single definition all the meanings attached to it (culture)."[9] James W. Carey,

7 Cf. "Kingship: Kingship in Sub Saharan Africa", in *Encyclopedia.com* updated 11 March 2020. Retrieved 15 February 2021. https://www.encyclopedia.com/environment/encyclopedias-almanacs-transcripts-and-maps/kingship-kingship-sub-saharan-africa

8 Renato Rosaldo, *Foreword. Defining culture*, in John Baldwin et al., *Redefining culture: Perspectives across the disciplines*, Lawrence Erlbaum Associates, New Jersey, 2006, p. xii.

9 Gottfried Lang, *Culture*, in Thomson Carson - Joan Cerrito, *New Catholic Encyclopedia*, vol

the American communication expert, thinks that culture is best understood in terms of "multiple realities," "a multiplicity of complex conceptual structures," "heterogeneous system of symbols," and "varying systems of meanings." And that is why he concludes that culture is "the result of complex, meaningful transactions," the process by which human beings create reality.[10] Culture makes reality for any group of people because it is through their culture that life has meaning. So, culture is an omnibus concept which involves all significant human acts, everything which gives meaning to a people. That is why culture does not just happen and it is not just wiped out. Culture is that life wire which has held a society from one generation to another.

In traditional Bamenda, culture is the unwritten covenant between the ancestors and the society; the bond between the living and the living-dead. Culture is sacred and inviolable. That is why, the Fon who is the personal manifestation of the bond and sacredness of the covenant between the people and their ancestors, is primarily the custodian of culture. One who owns his personal property is free to do whatever he chooses with it, but someone who has been solemnly entrusted with a property, does not have that kind freedom. He is just a custodian.

A custodian is given a moral obligation to guard, promote and keep a property that does not belong to him as an individual. It is in this way that the people of Bamenda speak of the Fon as the custodian of culture. He does not have the right to divert from what he received from others back to the ancestors. Hence in traditional Bamenda, culture is a matter of life and death, a covenant that is never compromised; and the Fon incarnates culture. In fact, he is seen as the highest ethnic instance and living manifestation of **Neutrality** and the **Common Good**.

5) The Fon as Symbol of Neutrality and the Common Good

A neutral person has no preferences, at least not publicly; he is impartial, objective and does not either lean towards or take sides with any party, especially in a conflict. It is in this way that the Fon is seen as a symbol of neutrality because, he is "father" to all the people under his care. He has no favourites and even if he feels for one more than the other, he is not allowed to give signs which will show that as Fon, he prefers one person over the other. The Fon simply seeks the common good. According to Waheed Hussain,

> "In ordinary political discourse, the 'common good' refers to those

4, Washington, Thomson Gale, 2003, p. 426.

10 Cf. James W. Carey, *Communication as culture,* Routledge, London, 2009, p. 20.

facilities - whether material, cultural or institutional - that the members of a community provide to all members in order to fulfill a relational obligation they all have to care for certain interests that they have in common. Some canonical examples of the common good in a modern liberal democracy include: the road system; police protection and public safety; courts and the judicial system;

public schools; cultural institutions; public transportation; civil liberties, such as the freedom of speech and the freedom of association; the system of property; clean air and clean water; and national defense."[11]

The relevant facilities and interests together constitute the common good and serve as a shared standpoint for political deliberation. In any community, the common good consists of the facilities and interests that members have a special obligation to care about in virtue of the fact that they stand in a certain relationship with one another. In a family, for instance, the home is part of the common good because the familial bond requires members to take care of the home as part of a shared effort to care for one another's interests in shelter and safety.[12] As the father, the bond and the custodian of an ethnic group, the Fon in traditional Bamenda is obligatorily always guided by the Common Good which is best for his people and for the ancestors. In this way, the Fon does not easily compromise with the *modus operandi* of his predecessors. He does not act in ways that are dubious; on the contrary, the Fon is clear as to what is good for his society.

These five aforementioned elements which mark the institution of Fon, show that the Fon ***is not just an ordinary person***. He is "divine" and receives both the protection and inspiration of the Ancestors. As Fon, the person who incarnates this institution is surrounded by a council of elders who make sure that the right things are done. Only in this way can we understand the Divine Authority of the Fon.

b) The Divine Authority of the Fon

Many people today think of "authority" in exclusively political terms, but authority is basically divine, the reason why St Paul tells us that *all authority*

11 Waheed Hussain, "The Common Good," in *Stanford Encyclopedia of Philosophy*, 2018, https:// plato.stanford.edu/ entries/common-good/, Retrieved 20 February 2021.

12 *Ibidem.*

comes from God (cf. Rom 13:1). We have all been created by God in His own Image and Likeness, and given husbandry of the universe and all its resources. Precisely, because we are different, yet with the same goal in life, we need a coordinating factor to bring together all the differences towards the one goal that we all have - to return to the same God who created us. That is why every authority must be seen in the light of the divine because the drama of our entire life unfolds in the presence of God; hence all good authority participates in, and derives its legitimacy from God.

The word *authority* derives from the Latin *auctor, auctoritatis* meaning the influence which one or more persons have over others. Therefore, in ancient Rome, although *auctoritas* referred to the general level of prestige a person had, and his influence and ability to rally support around his will, *auctoritas* was not merely political; it had a numinous content and symbolized the mysterious "power of command". That is why the Emperor, considered as the first citizen of Rome, (the *Princeps*) had what was then known as the *Auctoritas Principis* (the authority of the First Citizen). This was seen as the *supreme moral authority* in the State. Hence, ***authority*** was different from, but in conjunction with the *imperium* and *potestas* understood as military, judiciary and administrative powers.[13]

The 20th century German born American political scientist, Hannah Arendt equally considered *auctoritas* as the source of political authority and the continuous conservation and increase of principles handed down.[14] Noble men and women were expected to exercise more of *auctoritas* not *imperium* or *potestas*. It is in this sense that we are to understand Frank Bealey when he defines authority as "the legitimate power that a person or a group of persons consensually possess and practice over other people."[15] This is the proper understanding of authority – a divine privilege given to an individual or group of people to facilitate living together. It is in this way that we are to understand the "Divine Authority of the Fon" in traditional Bamenda. People listen to this authority because they feel that the Fon is worthy of respect. Generally speaking, people perceive the objectives and demands of such an authority figure as reasonable and beneficial, or true. Therefore, when we talk about the divine authority of the Fon it is to be understood that there are other types of authority.

13 Cf. James Bradstreet Greenough, "Latin Etymologies," in *Harvard Studies in Classical Philology*, Vol. 4, Harvard, 1893.

14 Cf. Hannah Arendt, *On Revolution*, Faber & Faber, London, 1963, Chp. 5.

15 Frank Bealey, *The Blackwell Dictionary of Political Science: A User's Guide to Its Terms*, Blackwell Publishing, New Jersey, 1999, pp. 22–23.

1) Types of Authority

The American Sociologist, Maximilian Karl Emil Weber, identifies three types of authority – traditional, political, and charismatic. By "traditional authority," he means that which derives from long-established customs, habits and social structures and handed down from one generation to another.

"Political" or "legal authority" is that which one gains through formal rules and established laws of the state, or it can also be a power which one seizes by power and imposes legitimacy on it. "Charismatic authority" or "Personal authority" derives from the moral uprightness which the person often claims to have received from a superior or more sublime source.[16]

The Fon in Bamenda is supposed to have all the three - traditional, legal, and much more charismatic authority. His traditional authority derives from his ancestors and the world of the spirits that has been handed to him from generations past. So, the Fon is aware that his authority comes from the gods. Then he needs legality by which he is chosen as the rightful heir, by the reigning Fon and the *Fon-makers*.

The idea of taking power by force is out of question given the ritual that has to be followed before he is finally declared Fon in traditional Bamenda. That is why the recent move by civil and political authorities to influence and precipitate the "election" of "*chefs traditionnels*" (traditional rulers) goes completely against cultural legitimacy. The Fon in traditional Bamenda merits the choice of the former Fon and the elders. That is why they must all be in agreement before a new Fon is chosen and enthroned. The individual to be chosen must have Charismatic or Personal authority – a good, God-fearing, and responsible person who has the common good at heart. These are the factors which give the Fon in traditional Bamenda, his "divine authority," especially as the Fon is primarily a High Priest.

2) Authority over the Temporal Goods of the Community

The concept and reality of "temporal goods" is very ecclesiastical, particularly with reference to the Catholic Church which sees the salvation of humanity as her real good, and every other material thing she owns as temporal. A Catholic priest is not ordained to administer schools, parishes, projects and so on; he is ordained to administer the sacraments and to teach the doctrine. However, since the Church is at the same time a human and divine institution, there are

16 Cf. Max Weber, *Rationalism and Modern Society*, translated and edited by Tony Waters and Dagmar Waters, Palgrave Books, 2015, pp. 136 .

necessary goods which she must own. Hence the Church sees in schools, a privileged milieu for evangelization and she owns health and social facilities for the good of the people who are being evangelized. Therefore, by virtue of being priest with a pastoral charge of people in a particular parish circumscription, the priest has a moral obligation to administer the temporal goods of the Church since these goods help her to carry out evangelization in a freer and more independent manner.

According to Canon 1496, all ecclesiastical goods must always be used for the purposes that allow the Church to possess temporal goods, namely: The organisation of worship services, the worthy support of the clergy and the promotion of works of mercy and charity, in particular for the benefit of the poor. So as a priest, administration becomes part and parcel of his triple role to teach, to sanctify and to administer or govern. It is in this light that a priest could be considered an administrator, but basically, his role is to be a spiritual leader to help the people achieve salvation. In a similar manner, the Fon in traditional Bamenda is primarily enthroned as the High Priest and the liaison between the living and the living-dead, between the people and the Divine. This is his primary and almost exclusive mission; but to do this, he has to have authority over the land and over the people.

That is why, it is only by derivation that the Fon may be considered as an administrator. When the English in particular took over British Southern Cameroons, they were impressed by the neat organisation of traditional authority in the Western Grassfields of Cameroon (Northwest, West, and parts of Southwest Regions). In fact, we are told that the British were so excited that they created traditional chiefs in areas where there were none[17] because they considered all the local chiefs as *auxiliaries of administration* and that was part of the reason for the creation of the "West Cameroon House of Chiefs."[18]

The British who were accustomed with the British Royalty and the House of Lords, knew that these "chiefs" were to be consulted for their expertise in ruling the traditional people, but they could neither be manipulated nor worse, be used as political tools against the people. The British House of Lords is sacred and cannot be banalized. In a similar manner, the Fons in traditional Bamenda are sacred institutions that cannot and should not be balkanized for political gain.

17 Cf. Peter Geschiere, "Chiefs and Colonial Rule in Cameroon: Inventing Chieftaincy, French and British Style," in *Africa: Journal of the International African Institute*, vol 63, no, 2, 1993, pp. 152-1-175.

18 Cf. Bongfen Chem-Langhëe, "The Origins of the Southern Cameroons House of Chiefs" *Op.cit.*

Even when these Fons are to be considered as "auxiliaries of administration," the extent and limit of their authorities must be taken into consideration.

Figure 2.2. Symbols of Fons as custodians of the temporal goods

Every Fon is anointed with ***soil***, a sign that he has moral authority of the entire land of his people. He is the true ruler of the land (the *chef de terre*, to use a French expression which is current in Cameroon, although used in reference to the wrong people – DOs). But he must stay in the Ancestral Shrine to receive wisdom and the moral force of his forebears.

Again, this is the context within which a Fon operates in traditional Bamenda; it is the only way to see the Fon as a person with divine authority. His authority cannot therefore be considered in modern terms in the context of partisan politics, where authority is utilitarian and divides more easily than unites. In traditional Bamenda, no one "owns" the Fon more than the other; the Fon is "Father" to all. And that takes us into our third Chapter of this first part.

Chapter 3

THE FON AT THE HEART OF PUBLIC RELATIONS

Figure 3.1. HRH Fon Azefor of Nkwen

"Public Relations" is a current and very important phrase in *Management and Business Administration,* in companies and organisations. Yet, in its objective and meaning, public relations is an active and professional attempt to maintain good relationships and improve a favourable public image of a group, company or organisation. That is why today, in every company, Public Relations (PR) shapes **public** opinion of the organisation and increases awareness of its brand.[1]

In a similar way, in the Bamenda Grassfields the Fon who is seen as an embodiment of the people is at the heart of public relations. And the public relations of a Fon in Bamenda is acted out in five different circumstances: through intermediaries when talking to subjects; directly with other Fons, in true dialogue with civil authorities; as neutral judge in conflicts; and an actor for the Common

1 Cf. Robert L. Heath, *Handbook of Public Relations,* SAGE Publications Inc., California, 2001, pp. 102-104.

Good of the people.

a) Fon Relating through Intermediaries

In traditional Bamenda, only two categories of people can talk directly to the Fon - those who have performed the official ritual of "greeting the Fon," and other Fons or people with similar ranks in their own society.

In Nso' for example, a mature adult can perform a special ceremony *(kimbun)* of bringing calabashes of palm wine, goats/fowls, firewood and other gifts to lobby the royal elders who then organise an official event during which the aspirant publicly "greets" the Fon. He then acquires the right to always greet him and any other Fon as well as be able to converse directly with any Fon. Otherwise, only other Fons and the royal elders[2] speak directly to the Fon. He speaks to others through an interpreter, even when "they" speak a language known and understood by the target audience. This way of relating to subjects clearly indicates that the Fon is not just an ordinary person; he is divine and as such is approached via intermediaries.

b) Relating with other Fons

Royal protocol in traditional Bamenda is very intriguing. These days, there are so many "Fons" (Chiefs) but they all know themselves and know their ranks. Five in the Northwest Region distinguished themselves and are accepted as "first class"- the *Fon of Nso', the Fon of Kom, the Fon of Bafut, the Fon of Bali* and the *Fon of Mankon.* These interact easily among themselves, shake hands and could even call each other in an eponymous manner.

Tributary Fons (who we would prefer to call *Chiefs*) do not have the same kind of privilege when dealing with these five first class Fons. None of these "chiefs" can sit to the right of any of the five "Fons" nor would they offer a handshake to them. On the contrary, they refer to these five as "our fathers" and they do not enter into any competition with anyone else in the Bamenda Grassfields. However, the "chiefs" can relate freely with each other but each is always conscious of his status and rank when all of them are together.

No matter the rank of any civil administrator appointed to the land of any of the five Fons of traditional Bamenda, the Fon retains his primacy and is ready to offer assistance if consulted. The British administrators to Southern Cameroons understood this *modus operandi,* and treated traditional authority with deep

2 Catholic Priests and Religious as well as sons of the land who have made great achievements are equally given this privilege.

respect. The colonial administrators could convoke one of these Fons but only when matters were very serious and, even then, the British always treated them with the deepest respect.

c) Relating through the House of Chiefs

We already made reference to a more detailed and historical research on the *House of Chiefs* in 1983, by Prof. Bongfen Chem-Langhëe.[3] Therefore we shall only highlight two important facts here.

First, the *House of Chiefs* was a meeting place where *Fons* and other traditional leaders met to discuss cultural issues and how they were to relate with the political society. The five Fons of Nso', Bali, Bafut, Kom and Mankon were *de facto* members (given the population they ruled) before others were considered.

The *House of Fons* and *Chiefs* was never influenced by any Minister or Government official, nor did any Fon publicly declare himself as a member of this or that political party, precisely because each Fon was always conscious of their role as neutral referees and "Father" to all. As we mentioned earlier, NO ONE "owns" the Fon in traditional Bamenda. So, the primary function of the Fon in the *House of Chiefs*, was to express cultural, historical and/or ethnic points of view on public policies. As custodians of the culture who knew that the identity and dignity of different groups depended on their respect for the patrimony of their ancestors, the Fons unequivocally took a preferential option for the common good of their respective groups. Nothing imaginable could have made a Fon (father of the people) to act against the very people over whom the ancestors gave husbandry.

Second, the Fons in the *House of Chiefs* understood themselves and acted as ***advisers*** to various administrators on matters of how to ensure unity, justice and peace in society. And none of the administrators (colonial or local) either doubted or tried to manipulate the authority of these Fons within their community. That is why, it would have been unthinkable that a "District Officer" (DO), a "Senior Divisional Officer" (SDO), a "Governor", or even a Minister could attempt to downgrade or belittle a Fon in his Fondom. Such an act would have been considered a cultural sacrilege. That is why all government administrators had the joy of creating, developing and reinforcing cordial relations with the Fon in each Fondom. In fact, one of the earliest acts of any civil administrator to a Fondom was to meet and introduce himself to the Fon with whom he would work in the governance of the people.

Each respected the status and dignity of the other, and that is how in truth,

3 Bongfen Chem-Langhëe "The Origins of the Southern Cameroons House of Chiefs" *Op.Cit.*

the Fons functioned well in the *House of Chiefs* as real advisers (*auxiliaries*) of administration. Since both the civil administration and the Fons understood their roles and status in society, there was hardly any conflict. So, the *House of Chiefs* was really a house where the *Fons* and the Chiefs discussed issues of common interest and from the vantage point of knowing the culture of the people.[4] The *House of Chiefs* also provided the right milieu for Fons to discuss how to handle internal and inter-group conflicts. Each Fon was aware of the expectations of the people when he was to arbitrate over any conflict.

d) The Role of the Fon in Conflict and War

The history of traditional Bamenda is marked by numerous internal conflicts and inter-communal wars.[5] Among some of the most notorious were the Bali-Bawock, the Bali-Ngyen-Mbo, the Kwashin and Mundali, the Bali-Kumbat-Bafanji, the Bambili-Babanki, the Babessi-Bambalang, the Mbesa-Oku and so on.[6]

Although these conflicts were inter-communal, there were also internal conflicts like the one following the disappearance of Fon Achirimbi II of Bafut on 14 December 1968 when a bloody antagonism arose over his succession.[7] In Kom, between 1958 and 1961, the women used their militancy (*Anlu*) to fight the rumour that their farmlands were about to be sold to rich Igbos. They also played a political role to dismantle the KNC (*Kamerun National Congress*) from power.

In each of these conflicts, we can see the major role played by the Fons and traditional rulers to bring about an end and reconciliation. For example, to resolve the inter-communal war between Bambili and Babanki, a meeting of neighbouring chiefs (the Fons of Bambili, Babanki-Tungoh, Bafut, Mankon and Nkwen) took place in the Bafut Council on 13 February 1965. Dr John Ngu Foncha, son of the area and Vice President of the Federal Republic of Cameroon

4 Cf. Bongfen Chem-Langhëe, *idem*.

5 Cf. Tangie Evelyn Ngengong, *From Friends to Enemies: Inter-Ethnic conflict amongst the Tikars of the Bamenda Grassfields (North West Province of Cameroon) C. 1950-1998,* M.A Thesis, unpublished, University of Tromso, Norway, 2007.

6 Cf. Patrick Bufang. *Inter-Chiefdom Conflicts in the North West Province of Cameroon from 1889-1999. Colonial and Post Colonial Influences,* Unpublished M.A, Thesis, University of Yaounde 1, 2000. Also see Divine F. Ngwa, *The Fon, Chiefs and People of Bafut in Conflict, Pre-colonial Period, 1968,* Unpublished DEA in History, University of Yaounde I, 2002.

7 Cf. Mark Bolak Funteh & Jean Gormo, "Women Conflict and Peace in the Grassfields of Cameroon," in *Africana Studia*, N°13, Universidade do Porto, 2009, pp. 91-113.

signed the agreements that were arrived at by the Fons.[8] In 2007, Fon Gilbert Njong of Mbesa and Fon Sintieh II of Oku also came together to resolve the 70-year old Mbesa-Oku conflict. Briefly, in almost all the conflicts in the Bamenda Grassfields, the Fons played a crucial and indispensable role in reconciling the people and bringing about peaceful co-existence.

According to Jude Waindim (2018), this is because the Fon is regarded with infinite respect and surrounded with carefully guarded secrecy. From his religious position, sitting on the ancestral chair and maintaining a nexus between his people and the ancestral spirits, the Fon *plays an instrumental role in the resolution of conflicts.*

Waindim rightly affirms that the Fon is both chief priest and custodian of all land, particularly so because he is considered to be an embodiment of the beliefs, hopes, fears and aspirations of his people. Thus, his judicial functions include reconciling human and spiritual forces.[9] That is why the role of the Fon in conflict resolution in traditional Bamenda, is always seen as that of a Father who is neutral, who listens to both sides and who is genuinely interested in establishing justice and peace among his children. Even when the issues concerned touch his own biological offspring, everyone expects the Fon to display almost divine neutrality, good sense of judgment and fairness towards all. In fact, it was always this expectation which made everyone in Bamenda to look on the Fon as the most trustworthy referee in every conflict. Whether they are present or not, the people know that their Fon will always negotiate for the common good.

e) The Fon Negotiates for the Common Good

Owing to his status as the "Father of His People," and his neutrality in arbitration, each Fon negotiates at every instance based on the principle of the Common Good, *that is to say, for the good of all and of each individual.* Since we are created as social beings, individual rights need to be experienced within the context of promotion of the common good; the "good that comes into existence in a community of solidarity among active, equal agents."[10] So, at no time will a Fon, in his right senses, ever take part in any act or decision that will stand against his people.

8 Cf. Tangie Evelyn Ngengong, *From Friends to Enemies: Inter-Ethnic conflict amongst the Tikars of the Bamenda Grassfield, Op. Cit.*

9 Cf. Jude Nsom Waindim, *Traditional Methods of Conflict Resolution. The Kom Experience,* in The African Centre for the Constructive Resolution of Disputes (ACCORD), No. 4, 2018.

10 John Paul II, *Sollicitudo Rei Socialis,* 30 December 1987, no. 38.

A **negotiation** is a process by which we arrive at an agreement by uncovering facts so as to better understand and share meaning thereby avoiding conflict. In any disagreement, individuals understandably aim to achieve the best possible outcome for their position (or perhaps the organisation they represent). In negotiation, we seek to understand and make the effort to be understood. A negotiation of necessity involves a dialectic between the different groups of people concerned. That is why the Fon who incarnates his people in traditional Bamenda must always engage only in dialogue, which is genuine and geared towards bringing real justice and peace. He is not interested in manipulations and tricks to exploit his subjects or those of his ethnic group.

This is because the status and role of the Fon in traditional Bamenda is so people-oriented that no one would expect him to behave otherwise. He must be interested in the common good and in justice to flourish in his land. In fact, we cannot properly understand any Fon in traditional Bamenda, unless we see him in the context of a "divine institution" acting as the liaison between the living and the living-dead. Only in this way can we begin to appreciate the difficulties brought to society today because some of our Fons are either being dragged or are personally making the effort to get fully involved in partisan and competitive politics. And that leads us into Part 2 of this work, which deals with ***Partisan Politics in contemporary Cameroon.***

PART 2

PARTISAN POLITICS IN CAMEROON

Figure 2A. Top left, Paul Biya (CPDM), Top right, Fru Ndi (SDF), bottom left, Maurice Kamto (CRM), bottom right, Adamu Ndam Njoya (UDC)

Since independence, Cameroon has been fluctuating between *monopartyism* and *multipartyism*. Following the birth of the SDF (Social Democratic Front) of Ni John Fru Ndi in 1990, the number of political parties in the country today beats the record. And so does the disagreements between them!

This second part of our work, presents in two chapters, the political evolution of Cameroon and explains why the involvement of the Fons of traditional Bamenda in this type of partisan politics constitutes a "cultural sacrilege." The first chapter of this part, Chapter 4 of the work, is a simple presentation of **The Evolution of Party Politics in Cameroon** between 1884 and 2020. At each level of evolution, the Fons always responded in such a way that their subjects were the beneficiaries. However, since 1992, the personal and deliberate involvement of some Fons, has raised a lot of dust. That is why Chapter 5 examines the reality of **Fons, Democracy and Partisan Politics in Cameroon**. The objective is to raise questions as to whether, given the facts as they are, the Fons in Traditional Bamenda should be involved in such political tussle for power. Reality and the human mind do not each create absurdity, but the *absurd* arises by the contradictory nature of the two, existing simultaneously.[1]

Figure 2B. L - Senator Fon Chafah III of Bangolan; R- Senator Fon Teche Njei of Ngyen-Muwa

1 Cf. Albert Camus, *The Myth of Sisyphus*, (tr. Justin O'Brien), Hamish Hamilton, London, 1955.

Chapter 4

THE EVOLUTION OF PARTY POLITICS IN CAMEROON (1884 -2020)

Figure 4.1. L- Ahmadou Ahidjo, pioneer president of Cameroon; R - Paul Biya, President, 1982-present

The evolution of party politics in Cameroon would make for a very exciting study and reading. Unfortunately, this work does not have the luxury of time. But suffice it to indicate that Tangie Nsoh Fonchingong has carried out some scientific research in that direction.[1] This chapter is only interested in an overview for the sake of justifying our thesis that the more the Fons got involved in partisan politics, the more they lost meaning and status. For this, we shall divide the history of party politics in Cameroon into five key moments.

The first moment presents multipartyism in *Kamerun* under the Germans

1 Cf. Tangie Nsoh Fonchingong, "Multipartyism and Democratization in Cameroon", *Journal of Third World Studies*, Vol 15, No. 2, 1998, pp. 119-136.

(1884-1916); the second examines another approach to multipartyism in Cameroun and in the Cameroons under French and British colonial rule (1916-1960). The third shows how the independent *Federal Republic of Cameroon* handled multipartyism (1961-66) while the fourth introduces us into the Single Party State (1966-90). Our fifth moment examines the return of a multiparty state (1990-2021). In each of these moments the Fons in Traditional Bamenda acted differently although it seemed clear with every change that they were drifting towards the present absurdity.

a) Multipartyism in Kamerun under the Germans

The Germans colonised *Kamerun* as one territory from 1884-1916. In fact, although Dr Max Butcher was sent as a Consul, it was only after the Berlin Conference (November 1884-December 1885), that Bismarck seemed to have grudgingly accepted to govern Kamerun, which eventually included the northern parts of Gabon and the Congo, western parts of the Central African Republic, the southwestern parts of Chad and parts of Nigeria.

Kamerun was then made up of a series of traditional States governed by powerful Kings, Fons and Chiefs who knew their role and who governed with Divine authority - the liaison between the living and their ancestors. When the Germans came, they sided with some chiefs over others, and conflict broke out. In the traditional set up, each Fondom or Chiefdom was an independent state with roles clearly defined.

So, when King Duala Manga Bell made a pact with the foreigners and took sides with the Germans against the chiefs of Jos and Bonaberi, the "Duala Wars" ensued.[2] On 16 January 1889 Dr Eugen Zintgraff, a German explorer arrived in Bali where he stayed for four months and built a German station. He signed a blood pact of friendship with Galega I and also took a Bali woman as wife. So, when Zintgraff visited Bafut later in 1889 and belittled the Bafut Fon, Galega was blamed for instigating Zintgraff to behave in this manner and trouble began. Sixteen years later, on 15 June 1905, another German mistake led to conflict. The German General Hauptmann Glauning formally installed Fonyonga II at Bali as paramount chief of 31 non-Bali villages in the assembly of 47 Grassfields Fons who unanimously rebelled and inter-communal wars ensued.[3] Such actions by

2 Cf. Victor Ngoh, *The Political Evolution of Cameroon,1884-1961*, Unpublished M.A Thesis, University of Portland, Dissertations and Theses, Paper 2929, 1979.

3 Cf. Jude Fokwang, *Historical Background to the Chiefdom of Bali Nyonga*, University of Pretoria ETD, 2003.

the Germans made them very unpopular to the local population.

The "natives" simply resented the rule of these foreigners and so, at the instigations of their Fons, they fought against the Germans in Mankon on the night of 10th December 1891, then in Bafut (1901-7) when the Commander von Pavel raided the palace of Fon Abumbi I several times.[4] The people of Fontem were up against the Germans in 1902; those of Mamfe from 1904-8; in Kom, the people fought from 1904-5; and Captain Glauning invaded Nso' in 1906.

In each of the situations, the people listened to their Fon and acted as instructed. The Fon was a divine figure and an incarnation of all that the Ancestors desire, so the people of traditional Bamenda spontaneously listened to their paramount leaders. And each Fondom was a very peculiar mix of monarchy and democracy.

b) Multipartyism Under the French and the British

After the defeat of the Germans during the First World War, Kamerun was divided into two, between the French and British, each piece given as a Mandate of the "League of Nations" (1922) and later as a Trust Territory of the UN (1946). The French section was called French Cameroun while the British was referred to as British Cameroons.

The manner in which these colonial powers treated traditional authority is very telling and gives reason for our worries in the present work. Also, during this time when political parties were still in their "seeding" phase, it is equally interesting to note the cautious attitude of Chiefs and Fons.

According to Prof. Verkijika G. Fanso, "when the French acquired their own portion of Cameroun after the partition of 1916, they decided to give temporary recognition to the judicial powers of the traditional chiefs."[5] But this lasted only until 1922 when the French made a full scale reorganization of the chieftaincies. For example, they rewarded the loyalty of a Beti elite, Charles Atangana, by making him "provincial Chief over the Ewondo and Bane groups."

In almost the same breath, they did everything to trim the overwhelming authority of Sultan Njoya in Bamum Kingdom. They created over fifteen local

4 Cf. Mathew Basung Gwanfogbe, "Resistance to European Penetration into Africa: The case of the North West Region of Cameroon" in *Journal of the Cameroon Academy of Science*, Vol. 13, No. 3, 2017.

5 Verkijika G. Fanso, *Cameroon History for Secondary Schools and Colleges. From Prehistoric Times to the Twenty First Century*, Revised Edition, Team Work Press, Bamkikaiy, Kumbo, 2017, p. 220.

chieftaincies in Bamum land and appointed people as chiefs who would be directly responsible to the administration, not to Njoya. When all of this failed to topple him, the French exiled Njoya to Yaounde where he died in 1933. Then the French went on to create three categories of chiefs – first class (lamidos, sultans and paramount chiefs - *chefs supérieurs*); second class (other chiefs appointed by or subordinate to the first class chiefs), and finally third class (village and quarter leaders). And from hence "traditional chiefdom" gave way to "administrative chiefdom" and the idea of "Chiefs" as "auxiliaries of administration" strongly came to the forefront. [6]

On the political scene, the idea of political parties was not yet well-developed in French Cameroun, although there were some revolts and tendencies against the colonial masters.[7] The dramatic climax however, came on 10 April 1948 when Charles Assalé, Ruben Um Nyobe, Ernest Ouandie, Albert Kinge and later Dr. Félix-Roland Moumié formed the UPC (Union des Populations du Cameroun), with clear objectives to fight for the total independence of Cameroun and for the reunification of French Cameroun with British Cameroon. But, since the UPC had Marxist tendencies, the French instigated other Camerounians against it. And so, to counter the influence of the UPC in the Bamileke area, a pro-government party, the Union Bamileke was founded in 1948.

Other groups like the "Evolution Sociale Camerounaise" (ESOCAM) was formed by some Bassa in 1949 and the "Renaissance Camerounaise" at Abong-Mbang.[8] Then Dr Paul Aujoulat and Andre-Marie Mbida founded the "Bloc Democratique Camerounais" (BDC) and in the North, Ahmadou Ahidjo created the UC (Union Camerounaise). But all these parties seemed to have one target – to fight against the UPC which was finally banned on 13 July 1955 and its leaders escaped to British Cameroons. UPC members were branded "Marquis" or terrorists; so, most of them went underground except a few including Ndeh Ntumazah and Bidjoka who instead created the One Kamerun Party (OKP) in 1957 and operated with UPC ideologies in and from Southern Cameroons.

On 15 May 1957, Andre Mbida of the Parti des Démocrates became Prime Minister of East Cameroun, but did not last for long as he had to resign on 18 February 1958. Ahidjo took over and Mbida escaped to Conakry, Guinea in 1959. So, virtually only one serious political party – the UC of Ahmadou Ahidjo

6 Cf. *Ibidem*, pp. 222-223.

7 Cf. Victor Julius Ngoh, *The Political Evolution of Cameroon, 1884-1961*, Unpublished M.A Thesis, University of Portland, Dissertations and Theses, Paper 2929, 1979, pp. 55-5.

8 *Ibidem*, p. 56.

- was left in East Cameroun when on 1 January 1960 with Dag Hammarskjold as representative of the UN, East Cameroun was declared an independent State, under the name "La Republique du Cameroun."[9] However, Ahidjo was aware that there were still smothering of partisan feelings other than that of the UC. In September 1960, during the third ordinary congress of the Union Camerounaise, Ahmadou Ahidjo therefore appealed for the building of a great national party. He asked the Mouvement d'Action Nationale du Cameroun (MANC) of Charles Assalé, and the regional association, the Union Tribal Bantou, which supported Assalé, to join the ranks of the Union Camerounaise.

We can therefore say that while in French Cameroun, the Chiefs "traditional chiefs" were transformed into "administrative chiefs" for political reasons; and while practically all the parties in this part were expected to subsume in the Union Camerounaise of Ahidjo, the story was different in British Cameroons.

The British introduced "indirect rule" with "local chieftaincies ruling the principal 'tribes' such as in Buea, Victoria and in the Grassland where the traditional chiefs exercised great authority."[10] There were Native Authorities (N.A.) administered by the chiefs who had competencies in judging and settling boundary, land and other disputes among the people. They also supervised development projects and organised the collection of taxes. In the 1920s and 1930s for example, the British established three administrative Native Authorities in Victoria, nineteen in Kumba, eight in Mamfe, and fifteen in Bamenda. The three NA in Victoria Division, each aided by an advisory clan council, were Chief Endeley of Buea, Chief Manga Williams of Victoria, and Chief Mukete of Muyuka. In Bamenda, four of these Native Authorities were the paramount Fons of Nso', Kom, Bali Nyonga and Bum. The Bafut Native Authority brought together some large chieftaincies, while the Fon of Bangwa (Fontem) was the only Native Authority in his own right in Mamfe Division.[11] All in all, the British recognised, respected and made use of the local chiefs to a point where they created a "Southern Cameroons House of Chiefs" to enable the local leaders discuss social, economic and cultural issues from their perspective without any partisan political influence.

The British were very wise because the trusteeship period witnessed a great deal of political development and the formation of political parties by Southern Cameroonians especially by those who were in Nigeria. Nerius Mbile and Robert Jabea Kum Dibongue created the Kamerun United National Congress (KUNC)

9 *Ibid*, p. 75.

10 *Ibidem*.

11 Cf. V.G. Fanso, *Supra*, pp. 238-240.

in August 1951 seeking the union of Cameroon, for which they made several unfruitful contacts with the UPC leaders. Most of the other Southern Cameroonians were members of the National Council of Nigeria and of the Cameroons (NCNC) which had been formed in Nigeria with Nnamdi Azikiwe. This party went into crises in 1953, forcing the politicians from the Cameroons to stage the historic walk out of the Eastern House in Enugu. Later, these Cameroonians organised a congress in Mamfe from 22-25 May 1953 and came out instead, with a petition requesting the creation of a separate autonomous legislature for Southern Cameroons. In fact, they were all united on this that from June 1953, all the political associations in Southern Cameroons had decided to merge to form one political party, the Kamerun National Congress (KNC).[12]

This was the first real Southern Cameroons political party with R.J.K, Dibonge elected as the President General and Dr Endeley as the leader of the parliamentary wing. Mbile opposed this merger and teamed with P.M. Kale to form the Kamerun People's Party (KPP) in 1953 as the second political party of Southern Cameroons. In 1955, when they saw that the KNC was no longer advocating for secession from Nigeria, two prominent members, Dr John Ngu Foncha and Augustine Ngom Jua resigned and founded the KNDP (Kamerun National Democratic Party).[13]

In 1957, Solomon Tandeng Muna resigned from the KNC and joined Foncha and Jua. The KNDP soon became the largest political party in Southern Cameroons. When the territory was uplifted in 1959 to full regional autonomy, the KNDP won 14 of the 26 seats in parliament. and ably formed a government while the KNC and KPP came together to form an opposition alliance in May 1960, called the Cameroons People National Convention (CPNC). Three other political parties in Southern Cameroons worth noting were the UPC (banned by the British in 1957 but acting underground), the One Kamerum (OK considered as the old UPC in disguise) of Ndeh Ntumazah and the Kamerun United Party (KUP) of P.M Kale with the sole interest of asking for the independence of Southern Cameroons as a sovereign State on its own.[14]

With Nigeria's independence on 1 October 1960, an interim Constitutional Order was introduced in Southern Cameroons pending a plebiscite. This Order endorsed the size of the Southern Cameroons House of Assembly and the House of Chiefs. It also gave the territory a separate judiciary, control over the police

12 Cf. V.G, Fanso, *Op.Cit,* pp. 298-299.

13 Cf. *Ibidem*, pp. 300-301.

14 Cf. *Ibidem*, pp. 301-302.

and other territorial affairs. Then talks about independence became louder and louder with Ahidjo trying to woo both Foncha and the KNDP on the one hand, and others believing in a totally separate and independent State of Southern Cameroons. The UN did not give this alternative, and the KNDP of Foncha convinced most of the people of Southern Cameroons to join La République du Cameroun and give birth to the Federal Republic of Cameroon – a new independent country with two States, under a single President. The Fons of traditional Bamenda who hitherto steered clear of partisan politics, agreed to this marriage because they trusted and respected Dr John Ngu Foncha and his KNDP.

c) Multipartyism in the Federal Republic of Cameroon

On 1 October 1961 the new Federal State was born. Article 1 of its Constitution read: "The Federal Republic of Cameroon is formed, as from 1 October 1961, of the territory of the Republic of Cameroun, henceforth called East Cameroun, and the territory of Southern Cameroons, formerly under the United Kingdom administration, henceforth called West Cameroon."

Practically speaking, the important political parties in the new Federal Republic of Cameroon, were the Union Camerounaise (UC) of Ahmadou Ahidjo and the Kamerun National Democratic Party (KNDP of Dr John Ngu Foncha. However, by November 1961, Ahidjo already began talking about the need for a "national united group" and a coordinating committee in the Federal House of Assembly. Although he had asked the MANC of Charles Assalé in 1960 to join his UC and although the UPC had been banned, Assalé was still reluctant to dissolve his party, but Ahidjo now put such pressure on him that on 8 September 1962, Assalé officially dissolved the MANC and called on the members to join the Union Camerounaise. He awarded Assalé with the post of the Prime Minister in the first Ahidjo government. Ahidjo also appointed Kamdem Ninyim of the Front Populaire pour L'Unité et la Paix (FPUP), Victor Kamga and Happi Louis Kemayou, both from opposition parties in order to woo more politicians into his UC solid base.[15] The UPC however, proved a hard nut to crack and it continued to operate underground. So, during the UPC Congress in Yaounde, Ahidjo sent police on 22 January 1962 to brutally disperse the members and arrest some.[16]

On 12 March 1962, Ahidjo issued a decree that prevented criticism against

15 Cf. Joseph Takougang, "The Post-Ahidjo Era in Cameroon. Continuity and Change" in *Journal of Third World Studies*, vol. 10, no. 2, 1993, pp. 270-71.

16 Cf. Frank M. Stark, "Persuasion and Power in Cameroon" in *Canadian Journal of African Studies*, Vol 14, No. 2, 1980, pp. 273-293.

his regime and this threw a wet blanket on many political parties and coerced many to join the Union Camerounaise. Those who resisted and wanted to go their way, were squarely dealt with. That is how on 27 April 1962, opposition leaders like André Marie Mbida of the PDC, Marcel Bebey Eyidi of the Parti Travailliste Camerounais, Charles Okala of the Parti Socialiste Camerounais and Theodore Mayi Matip of the UPC, were arrested, imprisoned and told to toe the line.[17] Then on 11 June 1965, Ahidjo convened the Prime Ministers of the two Federated States and the leaders of the three West Cameroonian political parties in Yaoundé and drove home the necessity of a single party and need for a centralized control for the proper functioning of the Federal Republic of Cameroon.[18] And so began a new air and approach to party politics in post-independent Cameroon. The Fons in "traditional Bamenda" made their voices heard through the Southern Cameroons House of Chiefs" which had both constitutional recognition and respect.

d) The Single Party Under Ahidjo (1966-82)

The KNDP of Foncha gradually became the official voice of West Cameroon and the U.C of Ahidjo, that of East Cameroun.

However, Ahidjo worked hard for a merger of the two hoping to achieve what he always talked about - a "national united group." In fact, on 1 September 1966, President Ahmadou Ahidjo merged all other parties and created a unique party - the CNU (Cameroon National Union). According to Mark DeLancey, by this arrangement, if anyone wanted to be elected to the National Assembly, membership in the CNU was required.[19] Only one party existed and dictated Government policies and only one Trade Union for workers – National Union of Cameroon Workers – was allowed in the country. Its activities and officials were very much controlled by the CNU. In fact, the President of the Trade Union automatically became a member of the Central Committee of the CNU

17 Cf. David Mokam, "The Search for a Cameroonian Model of Democracy or the Search for the Domination of the State Party: 1966-2006 in *Open Edition Journals*, https://doi.org/10.4000/cea.533. Retrieved 15 March 2021.

18 Cf. Mbu Ettangondop, "Federalism in a one-party state" in Victor Ngoh, (Ed.), *Cameroon: From a federal to a unitary state, 1961-1972. A critical study,* Design House, Limbe, 2004, pp. 108-142.

19 Cf. Mark W. DeLancey (1987) The construction of the Cameroon political system: The Ahidjo years, 1958–1982, *Journal of Contemporary African Studies*, 6:1-2, 3-24, DOI: 10.1080/02589008708729465.

with a mission to encourage all workers to support the Government.[20] No one was allowed to publicly show a lack of support to government. So, for daring to do that, on 15 January 1971, Ernest Ouandie Vice President of the UPC was publicly executed in a firing squad in Bafoussam, and this was meant to silence anyone else who dared to oppose the regime. But Mayi Matip and others who were imprisoned in 1962, were released and Mayi Matip became the Vice President of the National Assembly, an encouragement to those who showed loyalty.

Then, to solidify this support for government and to ensure a more centralised base of authority, Ahidjo organised what came to be arguably called the "Peaceful Revolution." On 20 May 1972, a plebiscite gave the President the power (99.9%) to change the name of the country, after just 11 years of independence, from the Federal to the *United Republic of Cameroon.*

There was only one legitimate political party - the CNU, one trade union, and one approach to how Government policies were to be executed. Ahidjo argued that the *federal* nature of the State hindered development and national unity. But Ahidjo knew when and where to soften his attitude. As a "yerima" or son of a village "lamido" (Chief) in the North, he was very sensitive and knew from experience, the depth of authority which traditional rulers wielded over their people. So, Ahidjo respected the Fons in traditional Bamenda and depended very much on their advice in handling issues in the society. Yet he closed the Southern Cameroons House of Chiefs, arguing that since the federal status of the country had ended, everything related to it had to go. Ahidjo took it for granted that all the Fons in a single-party State, would support the President and the Government. They were *de facto*, members of the CNU like every other Cameroonian. In fact, the more educated Fons who were interested, were given posts of responsibility in government.[21]

To make sure that no one would stand up against his plans, Ahidjo used the police, the army, the Gendarmerie, the *Service de Documentation* (SEDOC), the *Brigardes Mixtes Mobiles* (BMM) to maintain State security through intimidation, and where necessary, torture. In this way, the single party was uncontested and anyone who dared to raise an alternative voice was crushed. In 1972, when Dr John Ngu Foncha, Ahidjo's former Vice President and other West Cameroonians attempted to think of an alternative party to the CNU, armed police were sent

20 Cf. Joseph Takougang, "The Post-Ahidjo Era in Cameroon. Continuity and Change" *Supra*, p. 273.

21 Cf. Paul Nchoji Nkwi, "Cameroon Grassfield Chiefs and Modern Politics," *Op.Cit*, pp. 112-113.

to disperse the meeting.[22]

In 1972, and again in 1973 when students at the University of Yaounde demonstrated against the Government, they were brutally quelled by the military. Then in 1976, some two thousand people were arrested in Douala for rising up against the regime while another student uprising in 1978 met with similar repression.[23] By now the message was clear to all: if anyone dared to think outside the box, the consequences were not palatable. So, everyone was willingly or not, a member of the CNU!

Ten years after, in 1982, shortly before Ahidjo would hand over power to Paul Biya, while the country was celebrating the 10th anniversary of the One Party State, Prof. Bernard Nso'kika Fonlon, dared to write a highly academic critique of the state of affairs, wondering aloud if Cameroonian politicians in particular, understood the full implications of what it meant to have a United Republic. Fonlon's write up was published as the *Preface* to the then very popular scientific magazine – ABBIA. It was entitled: *Res Una Publica*, a call for us to "pause and ponder" about the Common Good – that which would genuinely benefit the vast majority. Fonlon believed that most of the politicians, especially the power brokers, did not seem to grasp what was at stake although they were celebrating the "peaceful revolution" of Ahidjo with pomp and pageantry.[24]

In all of this, the Fons in traditional Bamenda maintained their authority and looked after their people. There was just one party and everyone was supposed to belong to it and abide by what was decided! So, the Fons were more concerned about cultural issues of their society.

e) The Single Party Under Paul Biya (1982-90)

On 4 November 1982, President Ahidjo took everyone by surprise, announcing his resignation as President because of his health. Paul Biya, then Prime Minister, took over in accordance with the Constitution. Two days later, on 6 November, Bello Bouba Maigari was appointed Prime Minister. In his oath of office, Paul Biya promised continuity. During his maiden tour of the Provinces, Paul Biya insisted on the unity of the country and condemned all forms of division. On 18 September 1983, while addressing the special congress of the CNU in Yaounde, Paul Biya was clear that "*Cameroonians were first of all*

22 Cf. Joseph Takoungang, *Op. Cit.*, p. 278.

23 Cf. *Ibidem*.

24 Cf. Bernard Fonlon, "Res Una Publica" in *ABBIA*, *Special Issue, Tenth Anniversary of the United Republic of Cameroon,* Nos 38-39-40, Yaounde, 1982, pp. 11-39.

Cameroonians before being Bamilekes, Ewondos, Fulbes, Bassas, Bulus, Doualas, Bakweris, Bayas, Massas or Makas. This means that Cameroonians are first of all Cameroonians, before being English-speaking or French-speaking, Christians, Muslims or animists."[25]

As a shrewd politician, Biya needed the support of the north with a huge population. He was aware that during the Ahidjo rule, the lamidos of Maroua and Ngaoundere were disenfranchised. And that was probably part of the reason why in August 1983 Biya divided the North into three Provinces with Maroua and Ngaoundere as the headquarters of the Far North and Adamawa Provinces respectively.

In line with his belief of a united Cameroon, Paul Biya signed a decree on 4 February 1984, changing the official name of Cameroon from the United Republic of Cameroon to the Republic of Cameroon (La République du Cameroun), which was the name taken up by French Cameroun when it became independent in 1960.

According to proponents of the name change, this was a manifestation that the bilingual Cameroon Republic had gone beyond "mere" national unity to a much "higher stage" of national integration. Opponents of the name change, especially Southern Cameroons nationalist movements, argued that the 1984 name change was a brazen attempt to erase the identity of English-speaking Cameroonians, and trample upon their history.[26] But there was little the people could do, since the state security was on maximum alert.

However, a coup d'état on 6 April 1984 from members of the Presidential Guards largely from the North, profoundly changed a lot in Biya's approach to unity along the Ahidjo lines of politics. During the 1985 CNU Congress in Bamenda, Paul Biya transformed the party into his Cameroon People's Democratic Movement (CPDM), *Rassemblement Démocratique du Peuple Camerounaise* (RDPC). There was a clear wind of change and more freedom of opinion, but the country remained a single party state with the CPDM now as the only political party.

In the first quarter of 1990, Yondo Mandengué Black, Albert Mukong, Anicet Ekanet and others were arrested in Douala, allegedly for having held illegal meetings and for having distributed tracts hostile to the Head of State and calling

25 Cf. *CNU, The New Deal Messages*, Editions SOPECAM, Yaounde, n.d. p. 252.

26 Cf. Dibussi Tande, *A Rose by Any Other Name: "United Republic of Cameroon" vs. "Republic of Cameroon."* 31 March 2006, https://www.dibussi.com/2006/03/a_rose_by_any_o.html, Retrieved 18 March 2021.

for violence.[27] But the real reasons given for the arrest were that the arrested persons wanted to form a political party; and this move was considered illegal as there was a *de facto* single party system in Cameroon.

These Cameroonians were tried before the military court so as to give credit to the official version for their arrest. It was also a way of dissuading any other person from embarking upon a move towards creating a political party to challenge the state party.[28] But this single party incubation was not to last for long.

On 6 May 1990 the proprietor of the Bamenda-based Ebibi Bookshop along the Commercial Avenue, Ni John Fru Ndi, defied all odds and launched his *Social Democratic Front* (SDF) amidst stiff government opposition, heavy military presence and crackdown. Six people are said to have been killed. Members of the CPDM came out in their numbers in different regions of the country to protest this audacity of the SDF, but ironically, this was to mark the beginning of another phase in the evolution of partisan politics in Cameroon.

f) Multiparty Politics Under Paul Biya (1990-2020)

During the June 28/July 1990 extraordinary session of the CPDM, President Biya surprised but alerted his militants to be ready for possible competition, and to learn to win always.[29] A few months later, on 19 December 1990, President Paul Biya signed *Law No. 90/056* organizing political parties and making Cameroon once more a multi-party state. It is on record that about 123 parties registered. [30] Today hardly anyone can say for certain how many political parties exist in the country.

The more popular parties which have registered and have been somewhat active include: the Cameroon People's Party (CPP) of Edith Kah Walla; the Cameroon Renaissance Movement (MRC) of Prof. Maurice Kamto; the Cameroon Democratic Union (UDC) of Adamou Ndam Njoya; the Cameroon Party for National Reconciliation (PCRN) of Cabral Libii; the Front for the National Salvation of Cameroon (FSNC) of Issa Tchiroma Bakary; the Movement for the Defence of the Republic (MDR) of Dakole Daissala; the Movement for the Liberation and Development of Cameroon (MLDC) of Marcel Yondo; the National

27 Cf. Zacharie Ngniman, *Cameroon - Politics and government – 1960 Politics and government Cameroon*, Edition CLE, Yaounde, 1993, p. 46. Also, Luc Sindjoun, *La Revolution Passive au Cameroun*, CODESRIA, Dakar, 1999, p. 86.

28 Cf. David Mokam, "The Search for a Cameroonian Model of Democracy" *Op.Cit.*, p. 22

29 Cf. *Cameroon Tribune,* N0.1033, 4 July 1990, p. 13.

30 Cf. Le Messager, No.480, 15 February 1996, p. 5.

Union for Democracy and Progress (UNDP) of Maigari Bello Bouba; the Progressive Movement (MP) of Jean-Jacques Ekindi and the Social Democratic Front (SDF) of Ni John Fru Ndi. Although registered as opposition parties, a good number of these, like the MDR, FSCN, and UNDP got into such alliance with the CPDM such that they could have been considered its satellites.

However, the interest of this chapter, as is the interest of this entire work, is not to study or analyse these political parties, but to indicate from their evolution that the thinking of many Cameroonians had changed enormously in the oscillation from multipartyism to single partyism. This influenced both the concept and status of the Fon in traditional Bamenda, which stood out as the one area which dictated political opinion and reaction. The way people think and act in a one party state is different from when they are in multipartyism.

The concept and reality of Fon in traditional Bamenda did not permit this institution to get involved in partisan politics because the Fon represented neutrality, justice and the Common Good.

However, in a one party state, it was easy for people to ignore, and not even get worried as to whether the Fon is meddling in politics since everyone was under the same party. But, in multiparty politics, people were and still are, most sensitive as to what their traditional rulers in general, and the Fons in particular, are doing politically. In fact, the political parties in West Cameroon, which won the support of the people, were those that respected the Fons as custodians of culture, not political tools. According to both Victor Le Vine and Victor Ngoh, "Dr. Endeley made many mistakes in dealing with the symbols and spokesmen of tradition in the territory. He would offend th*e 'Fons'* by shaking their hands, sitting at their side on stools reserved for other fellow *'fons'* or by addressing them by the wrong title or at the wrong time or for his haughtiness in *'spikin da big Inglish*." Foncha on the other hand, was extremely fluent in pidgin English and respected all the traditional norms."[31]

31 Cf. Victor Ngoh, *Op.cit*, pp. 82-90; Victor T. LeVine, *The Cameroon from Mandate to Independence,* University of California Press, 1964, p. 210.

Chapter 5

FONS, DEMOCRACY AND PARTISAN POLITICS IN CAMEROON (1992-2020)

Figure 5.1. L- HRH Fon Forchesiri III of Bamendankwe; R- Senator Mfon Victor Mukete

The concepts and reality of *"Democracy"* and *"Partisan Politics"* have such complex overtones in contemporary Cameroon that they can trigger any type of emotion, depending on the context and the person who uses these words. Yet the two terms have clear origins and objective meanings. This chapter wants to step out of emotionalism and examine first what these words mean, then how they are used in Cameroon, and what the implications are for the Fons in traditional Bamenda.

a) What is Democracy?

Our world is awash with cries for *democracy;* and America positions herself today as the great advocate for democracy, presented as the best government which respects basic human rights and freedoms. Yet the 2020 Presidential elections in the USA indicated to us that lies can overshadow democracy; that millions can be manipulated to act hysterically in the name of wanting to defend democracy. The excitability and emotion of people and their mass mobilization can indeed incite democracy to acts of hysteria. Our world is simply crazy about liberties and human rights. Even in a fairly young country like Cameroon, people proudly talk about and proclaim an "advanced democracy" (*une Democracie Advanceé*) which David Mokam and others call a "ruling democracy."[1] Yet this is nothing new because when Plato watched how "democracy" was practiced in Athens, he exclaimed : "*An excessive desire for liberty at the expense of everything else is what undermines democracy and leads to the demand for tyranny.*"[2] In using the word "Democracy" today, it seems that many of us are not aware of the hidden intricacies involved. What is democracy?

The term *democracy* first appeared in ancient Greek political and philosophical thought in the city-state of Athens during classical antiquity. In fact, our world was introduced to the word *democracy* via Plato in his *Republic*; and Plato's *Republic* is widely acknowledged as the cornerstone of Western Philosophy and the first great examination of political life.[3]

Democracy is a combination of two Greek words – *demos* (people) and *kratos* (rule); so etymologically, Democracy is said to be a *government of the people, for the people, by the people*; a government where the people choose who will rule them. In a democracy, ideally, the people make their voices heard, and they vote and get what they want. So, those who govern are accountable to the people and act solely for the Common Good. As an ideal, every citizen in a democratic state has equal rights and all share an equality in dignity as persons. Each individual matters and his opinion counts in a democracy. And this sounds like a very attractive and great inspiration to many people.

In fact, since 1990, the wave of democratic change has been sweeping throughout the whole world, including Africa in general and Cameroon in particular. The people want to be in charge of their destiny; they want to have a say in who is to rule them, so each vote should count and matter. At face value, democracy seems to be such a wonderful idea, but we need a more critical stance before we can understand that there is more than catches the eye.

Plato, the *Father of Politics*, watched the whimsical nature of public support; the manner in which the populace were manipulated against the wise Socrates and concluded that the majority view is not always the best. Therefore, Plato had

1 David Mokam, *Op.Cit.*, pp. 1-3.

2 Cf. Plato, *Republic*, Book VI.

3 Cf. Arc Ninian, *Why Plato Hated Democracy*, 12 June 2020, in https://aphilosophersstone.org/why-plato-hated-democracy-3221e7dcd96e. Retrieved 20 March 2021.

misgivings about democracy. Simple as it sounds, it would appear as the best form of government unless one stops and reads between the lines. If the people who are to vote are all of the same enlightenment and know what the implications are of their vote, then indeed Democracy can be a wonderful expression of the opinion of the majority; but if the majority of the people are barely literate and are easily manipulated, then democracy can become a vote by the ignorant.

In Book VI of the *Republic,* Plato states that if we want a good captain for a ship, we do not look at the popularity of a person or how much he owns, we rather look at the capacity of the person, his skill and experience in steering a ship, understanding weather and the necessary issues which go along with controlling a ship in the ocean. If people are simply asked to vote a captain and they do not know what it entails to steer a ship in the sea, they will go for the most popular person and the one who appeals to them. The majority may vote and win but their opinion is disastrous to the common good. And that is why Plato hated *Democracy* as a system of government.

Plato believed that the ***Philosopher-King*** must always rule. This is the one who will always ask the "whys" and get to the root-cause of issues. Using his analogy of the ship, Plato believed that " *the true navigator must study the seasons of the year, the sky, the stars, the winds, and all the other subjects appropriate to his profession if he is to be really fit to control the ship...*" The leader must of necessity be one who loves and goes after wisdom. And according to Plato, (in Book VII), this unencumbered love of wisdom negates the possibility of the love of falsehoods, physical pleasures, material pleasures, meanness, and cowardice, all desires and tendencies that threaten to corrupt leadership.

In his famous Allegory of the Cave (Book VI), Plato illustrates a moment in which a man discovers that the reality of the world is different from that perceived by the prisoners in a cave. As this man returns to the cave to reveal his discovery, he is met with violent rage.[4] This is very symbolic of what happened to Socrates in the city of Athens as he tried to get the youth to reason out their lives and live by conviction, not by emotions and manipulations.

b) Democracy in Cameroon

According to the British Professor of International Human Rights Law, Rachel Murray, there is no consensus about "a precise or even an appropriate working definition of what Africa perceives as democracy."[5] In an interview in

4 *Ibidem.*

5 Cf. Rachel Murray, *Human Rights in Africa. From OAU to the African Union*, Cambridge

2006, the then President of France, Jacques Chirac, publicly said: "Democracy is luxury for Africa."[6] According to the Cameroonian legal expert, Dr Michael A. Yanou, the word democracy is capable of multiple definitions, but often restricted to the context of governance in Cameroon, which assumes that democracy is desired by the people and attained through some form of elections that lead to the Cameroonian people having some ultimate authority.[7] However, if we were to judge democracy in Cameroon from the success or failure of organised elections, then there is still much homework to do to affirm the Cameroonian "advanced democracy." Even the Government appointed Election Observatory, ELECAM, suggested a reform to the electoral laws in 2012 and in 2020. Since 1990 after multiparty politics was re-introduced, there has hardly been any election in Cameroon that was not vigorously contested.

In a thought-provoking article: *Cameroon's Democratic Process: Vision 2020,* Mwalimu George Ngwane, did not mince words that democracy in Cameroon is limping. In his own words: "For more than a decade, the goals of multiparty democracy still elude the masses and within the present political context of unbridled demagogy, multiparty democracy may remain a façade and charade, promising much but delivering little."[8] Several experts have suggested different indicators to use to assess the quality and level of democracy in any country. Among these indicators, five are clearly common to all: *Free and Fair Elections, Alternation in People who hold Power, Freedom of the Press and Expression of Opinion, Accountability of Government Officials,* and *Neutrality of the Military.*[9] When these indicators, collectively or individually, are used to assess the quality of democracy in Cameroon, much is still left to be desired.

Fombad and Ewang have argued, for example, in the context of Cameroon, that limiting the evaluation of elections only to the outcome of the total votes does not give an accurate picture of democracy. According to them, it is also important to assess who organised the elections and how the final results were

---

University Press, Cambridge, 2004, p. 75.

6 Cf. Jacques Chirac, in Ouatttara, F. (2006). *Kant et la problématique de la promotion de la paix. Le conflit entre l'utopie, la nécessité et la réalité de la paix durable.* Unpublished Master dissertation, University of Ouagadougou, Ouagadougou, Burkina Faso. Http://www. memoireonline.com/

7 Cf. Michael A, Yanou, "Democracy in Cameroon. A Socio-Legal Appraisal," in *Verfassung und Recht in Übersee / Law and Politics in Africa, Asia and Latin America* , Vol 46, no. 3, 2013, p. 304.

8 Cf. George Ngwane, *Cameroon's Democratic Process: Vision 2020,* in https://www.gngwane.com/files/cameroons_democratic_process.pdf

9 Cf. National Democratic Institute (NDI), *Democratic Indicators,* Iraq, 4 April 2004.

obtained.[10] According to Michael Yanou, electoral institutions in Cameroon enjoy little or no confidence of the majority of the people.[11] About alternation in people who hold power, the facts where the same people have been recycled over and over, year in year out for four decades and more, makes it difficult to use this democratic indicator in Cameroon.

With regards to Freedom of the Press, Reporters Without Borders, in its 2020 *World Press Freedom Index,* ranked Cameroon 134th out of 180 countries in the World Press Freedom Index. Cameroonian journalists have been detained, some have died in detention, quite a few are in exile and some are on the run. About *Freedom of Expression,* the 2019 Human Rights Report states that although the Constitution and laws of the land provide for such freedom, individuals and groups which voice opinions contrary to government policies are often tracked down and penalized. The Report cites several instances where this concretely happened.[12]

The National *Anti-Corruption Commission* (*CONAC*) was established by the Presidential Decree No. 2006/088 (in French) of 11 March 2006, to fight corruption and ensure accountability of civil servants over husbandry of state patrimony. The institution has pointed to several state and parastatal organisations at the heart of great corruption and unaccountability. Even the Head of State has publicly decried the attitude of some of his ministers, over 10 of whom he has imprisoned in Kondengui for lack of accountability.

Finally, several Human Rights groups, NGOs and international bodies have called to question, the neutrality of the Cameroon military. The army spokesman had to react on several occasions, especially with regards to the role and action of the military, during the armed conflict in English-Speaking Cameroon (2016-2021).

c) The Fons and Multiparty Democracy in Cameroon

If *democracy* was understood and applied in its original meaning and ramifications, the Fons in traditional Bamenda would not only be right, but it would also be a moral obligation for them to be part of such a democracy. Unfortunately,

10 Cf. Charles M. Fombad & A.S. Ewang, "Election Management Bodies and Peace Building in Africa. Cameroon's Move from National Election Observatory (NEO) to Elections Cameroon (ELECAM)," in *Revue Africaine Des Sciences Juridiques,* no. 2, Yaounde, 2008, p. 2.

11 Cf. Michael Yanou, "Democracy in Cameroon," *Op. Cit.*, p. 313.

12 *Cameroon 2019 Human Rights Report,* in https://www.state.gov/wp-content/uploads/2020/03/CAMEROON-2019-HUMAN-RIGHTS-REPORT.pdf, Retrieved on 20 March 2021.

wishes are not always horses for beggars to ride! Yet some Fons have taken clearly compromising positions in partisan politics in Bamenda and this raises lots of moral, social and cultural problems. When a Fon, understood as a symbol of neutrality, clearly takes a partisan position, what happens to other subjects of his Fondom, who are militantly in opposition to the stand and policies of the party he supports? What kind of relationship can such a Fon have with such subjects? Can they sincerely trust each other?

Let us remind ourselves of the major premise when it concerns the Fons. The Fon in traditional Bamenda is primarily a High Priest installed to liaise between the living and the living-dead of the Fondom. His role is to unite, never to divide. Therefore, given the style of partisan politics that is operative in Cameroon, one wonders if a Fon should be involved in such filth and "game of interest."

When Plato saw what was happening in ancient Athens, in the name of democracy, he was convinced that the democratic man is more concerned with his money over how he can help the people. He does whatever he wants whenever he wants to do it. His life has no order or priority. The Greek authorities conspired and condemned Socrates to death, not because they were sincere in saying that he (Socrates) corrupted the youth, but because that was the emotional pretext to use against the philosopher. Give a dog a bad name and then kill it! They manipulated the Athenians to believe what was profoundly false. Should this be the role of the Fons?

The ancient Greeks believed very much in ***virtue***, especially among the elite and the educated. In fact, for good old Socrates, virtue and knowledge were so interwoven that one could not be without the other. Hence for him, virtue was knowledge. The presumption here is that a learned person knew by experience and theory what it meant to be good, hence, he more than anyone else was expected to be virtuous. Education is meant to make a human being more humane and a better "rational animal." When the human being allows his rational self to be more operative, he performs great and good acts; but when he allows the opposite to happen, horror strikes.

The elite, like the learned, are the leaders of the people and should be the most virtuous of people. That is why the ancient Romans who took over civilization from the Greeks believed that the corruption of the good people, was the worst form of corruption. Hence the Latinists used to say: *Corruptio Optimi est pessima* (The Corruption of the Best, is the Worst of all). The Fons in traditional Bamenda are supposed to be the best by virtue of their link with the ancestors and by the mission that is incumbent on them as the traditional spiritual leaders of the people.

The British Medieval Poet, Geoffrey Chaucer makes a commentary in his *General Prologue* to the *Canterbury Tales,* about the Poor Parson, the village priest who lived a humble life doing good deeds in the community. The people believe and put their trust in him. So, Chaucer reminds the priest that he has to avoid all worldliness because "if gold rusts what would iron do?" because it is horrible to have a *"dirty (shitten) shepherd and clean sheep."*[13] The spiritual leader of the people must make effort to stand out. And this should take us to the last and more analytical part of this work - part 3.

13 Cf. Geoffrey Chaucer, *The General Prologue to the Cantebury Tales.*

PART 3

IN SEARCH FOR MEANING

Figure 3A. Using cowries to search for meaning

"Meaning" is one of those common words which people use daily but which they have difficulty in understanding and defining. Yet we live in a world where communication sciences influence, if not determine, much of what people think, say or do; and the concept of meaning is so central to communication, that it has become the core concern of human life today. People seek to understand why others act, speak or think the way they do. So, they are quick to ask each other:

"What is the meaning of this or that?" The question may appear very simple to the person asking but it is only deceptively simple.

Generally, *meaning* is the sense, the significance or whatever a thing or person intended to convey to another. But what is intended may not always be what is actually conveyed; and this raises the concept of "meaning" from an ordinary to a philosophical level.

Language philosophers of the early 20th century talked about two types of "Theories of Meaning" – the *Semantic* and *Foundational*. The *Semantic Theory of Meaning* looks at expressions and sentences as they are and interpret what these words say. For example, when I tell someone: "I am hungry" the person is expected to understand that "I have not eaten." But if my friend who knows that I have just eaten was there, he would have to understand something else. This is the *Foundational Theory of Meaning*, which is only understood when put in context. When Donald Trump, for example, told his supporters after the 2020 Presidential Elections in the USA that their "victory is being stolen," many journalists and Americans said that the President was lying because they were looking at the truth value and semantic meaning of what Trump said. But when language philosophers now analyse the statement of the former President in the light of all that happened, we can begin to understand what Trump actually intended; and millions of his supporters found meaning in what he said, and reacted the way he intended.

"Meaning" is that which makes sense and creates "reality," for a people. And reality is not something out there to be named and identified. "Reality is not there to discover in any significant detail." It is not "humanly existent, independent of language." In brief, we do not have some distinct thing called *reality* which exists of its own. On the contrary, "reality" is that which is brought into existence or created by humans.[1]

This third part of our work is a *search* for such *meaning* that would reconstruct reality and the lost identity of a people who always knew who they were, where they were going to and what they wanted until conflict and war destroyed their society. There is, therefore, a shouting need to make amends for the "cultural sacrilege" that was committed and to restore the expected cultural dignity and value, albeit, in a changing global village. A deeply rooted social crisis destroyed so much that reconstruction must begin by carrying out what Catholic Church scholars refer to as a *sanatio in radice* (healing from the roots). And the best root to tackle first, is the restoration of the identity, dignity and meaning of Fon in traditional Bamenda.

As we have already demonstrated, the Fons in traditional Bamenda had such meaning and identity that everyone who came into the area was never in any

1 Cf. James Carey, "A Cultural Approach to Communication," in *Communication*, vol. 2, no. 1, 1975, pp. 19-21.

doubt as to the deep significance of this institution to the people. But so many atrocities were committed that first, the ancestors await restitution. And this is the task of this part of our work.

It is an arduous task especially as majority of those who were responsible for the desolation and the *status quo* can hardly be blamed for their ignorance. A good number of those concerned with the cultural sacrilege, were young "cultural hybrids," some of them such "super-hybrids" that they had little or no cultural base. In addition to this, the key factors which contributed to the actual deconstruction of the institution of Fon, were neither clinically identified nor was there any genuine will to do so. That is the reason why in the following two chapters, we hope to redefine and reconstruct identities (Chapter 6) before making bold proposals in the last chapter (Chapter 7) about the restoration of the dignity of the Fon.

Chapter 6

RECONSTRUCTING IDENTITIES

Figure 6.1. Modernity and tradition can co-exist

Identity as a subject for analysis and discussion, and as a lived reality for all of us, has never been more complex and multifaceted as today. Uneven though they are, technological advances and globalization change the way people understand their identities. Social media, as a synthesis of both, shapes the identities of the groups we belong to and the identities of individuals and other groups that have hitherto existed beyond our view. Reflection on, and thoughtful reconstruction of identity exist side by side with simplistic and hostile categorization on *Facebook* and other social media.[1]

1 Cf. Nicolas Monk et al., *Reconstructing Identity. A Transdisciplinary Approach*, Springer Nature, Switzerland, 2017, p. 1.

The word "identity" includes the qualities, the experiences, memories, beliefs, personality, relationships and values that create a sense of self either to an individual or to a group. Hence, we talk about **personal** and **social identity,** each only understood in relation to the other. Once the essential elements of identity are destroyed or manipulated, the individual is the first victim and begins to grope through life, often living inauthentically. That is why most people and groups fight to protect their identities. In fact, many conflicts in the world have often been caused by attempts to attack, alter or destroy the identity of a people or individuals. The latter fight back with all energy, not prepared to let go the very elements which make them who they are. At the same time every conflict leaves in its throes issues of identity which cry out for urgent and meaningful reconstruction.

In this chapter we are faced with a people who were fighting to defend their identity, but an armed conflict ensued and left lots of issues in its backlash. The armed conflict in the Northwest and Southwest Regions of Cameroon was essentially a fight for an identity. The people of the former *Southern Cameroons* felt that their identity as a people who freely decided to join *La République du Cameroun* in 1961, was in danger of being assimilated. Simple as it looked, the manifestation of these feelings was allowed to be overridden by partisan emotions, and the situation degenerated into a senseless fratricidal war. One of the most painful casualties of the war was the sad reality that some Fons in traditional Bamenda compromised their divine mission as high priests and custodians of culture; and since the centre could not hold, things fell apart. Consequently, there was wanton destruction of ancestral shrines, arson in palaces and a downright rejection of the authority and dignity of some Fons.

As we have already indicated, a good number of those involved in this cultural sacrilege were youngsters for whom "patrimonies" and "legacies" meant little or nothing. These young people found on both sides of the war, were children of two worlds for whom history and anthropology are far-fetched sciences. But they were sponsored in some cases by people who should have known better! And once a human being allows emotions to ride over reason, then as the ancient Roman playwright Titus Maccius Plautus once wrote: *Homo lupus homini est* (Man becomes a wolf to his fellow man). This belief was shared and expanded upon by the 17th century English philosopher, Thomas Hobbes.[2] The human being is a rational animal, which means that when his rationality is operative, he

2 Cf. Thomas Hobbes, *Leviathan or The Matter, Forme, & Power of a Common-Wealth Ecclesiastical and Civill,* April 1665.

is the best animal on earth, but once the animal nature is given free vent, jungle law takes over. So, one of the basics we should understand about the human person is the fact that he oscillates between the two extremes of irrationality and rationality, building and destroying his own identity as he acts.

Culture is a core indicator and guarantee of human identity. However, in the changing world in which we live today, this culture can go through several upheavals affecting the identity of individuals and groups of people. And this is part of what happened in the case of the Fons in traditional Bamenda. To fully understand this, we would need to briefly consider and examine the concept and consequence of culture in a changing world.

a) Culture in a Changing Society

The American sociologist, Wendi Griswold published a book on 14 February 1998 entitled *Cultures and Societies in a Changing World.*[3] She states, as a matter of fact, that culture is a core concept and reality for each people, their identity which gives meaning to their lives. In the face of inevitable change and increasing globalisation, culture becomes a great receptacle as well as a determinant factor to the unchangeable variable. That is why although the culture of a people is very crucial to their identity, there is nothing like a "pure culture."

Cultures receive and give; they determine and are determined by change; and as things change, values and beliefs begin to shift ground. So, what our forebears believed in, will not necessarily be the same in our times. Three main factors often influence cultural change - *contact, technology* and *environmental factors.* When two cultures meet, each influences the other in a process of *cultural diffusion, integration, acculturation* or others. *Technology* is a very crucial factor which can easily change the culture of a people. For example, the cell phone has replaced the "talking drum" in the Northwest Region of Cameroon; the Internet has changed the mailing system and relationships between people. Brief, the digital era has profoundly changed the way in which people think, speak, act and relate to one another. The last main factor of cultural change are environmental causes. Today, we talk of the world as a global village; and this globalisation has had a huge impact on cultures. That is why cultures are always evolving; they are never static.

When something new opens up, new ways of living, and when new ideas enter a culture, there is bound to be change, no matter how slight. Cameroon

3 Cf. Wendi Griswold, *Cultures and Societies in a Changing World*, 4th Edition, Sage Publications, London, 2013.

has changed enormously since 1972, and this change has affected many areas of life, including the manner in which people live, believe and act. Hence, many cultural aspects and values have changed. Instead of ethnic traditional rulers, we inherited colonial systems of governance, some of which clash with the cultural systems we had been used to.[4]

Nonetheless, although change has become a constant in modern society, for every change, there is always the invariable which make it possible for us to still recognize what was, what is, and what will be. And the institution of Fon in traditional Bamenda is definitely one of those invariables in the discourse about the identity of the people. But if we are now concerned about change in the "unchangeable" it is because we allowed a number of avoidable factors to cause a change in the institution of Fonship. Three of these factors seem obvious - *the sustainability of the Fon*; *the invasion into our society of the idolatry of money*; and *the lack/non-respect of rules in our game of partisan politics.*

About fifty or more years ago, ethnic cohesion and identities were very strong. The Fon was the final authority and it was a pride, even a duty, for men to daily offer calabashes of palm wine, animals caught during organised hunting expeditions, and kola nuts harvested from family estates. So, the palace was something like a warehouse where food and drinks were kept to entertain strangers and visitors.

The palace women could count on cornflour and vegetable or *achu* brought to them by other women for entertainment. The palace was everyone's home and a refuge for anyone in problems. The children of the palace were sent to schools and colleges largely on scholarship or support from the subjects, so, the Fon had little or no burden to carry. As time went on, and people moved out of Fondoms looking for greener pastures, little was discussed concretely on how the Fon was to be sustained. Hence by sheer force of lack of means, the institution of Fon began feeling the pinch of having to manage a huge number of children, a bevy of wives and visitors who were probably not aware that the palace was now "dry". And that is why the question of the sustainability of the institution of Fon became pertinent.

In modern project management, people meticulously make sure that the factor of sustainability is concretely ensured or at least discussed to an extent that we are more or less sure of what results to expect. In fact, sustainable project

4 Cf. Smirti Chan, *Cultural Change: Main Factors and Causes of Cultural Change*, https://www.yourarticlelibrary.com/culture/cultural-change-main-factors-and-causes-of-cultural-change/23392. Retrieved 23 March 2021.

management has become central and a *conditio sine qua non* in business planning. Our Fondoms were not planned and as change stepped in, we did not seem to care much to discuss the issue of sustainability; and this was our Achilles' heel! Added to this lack of sustainable management of our Fondoms, was the apparent irresistible lure and attraction for money; that tainted thing which easily corrupts the soul, and becomes the source of all evil (1 Tim 6:10). In our modern world, money is key to survival and development. Vikas S. Shan, an award winning entrepreneur firmly believes that "*it is difficult to underplay the profound importance of money in the human story,*" because without money today, we can do little.[5]

In a world where money is given such central importance, the English are right to tell us that "*He who pays the piper calls the tune.*" The Fon cannot do without money in our modern and changing world. And because in most Fondoms, even the elite seemed to have forgotten the Fon in this respect, the need for money became one of the in-routes through which the unscrupulous came into the scene and manipulated, raped and took away the real authority and dignity of the *Fons*. Perhaps in a situation where rules clearly define the contours of each game, it would have still been able to salvage our *Fons,* but in the game of our partisan politics, either such rules are absent or simply not being followed.

In England, one of the greatest monarchies in the contemporary world, royalty is respected and never to be hijacked by any political party. Every English person knows that as one of the canons of being English. That is why the House of Lords, after which our former Southern Cameroons House of Chiefs was patterned, can still remain, even today, a credible advisory body and mediator in English politics. On the contrary, in our manner of doing partisan politics, the rules (if there are any) do not seem to clearly define the extent and limits of each party and each individual. There is such an open field that anyone does as he wants, and is capable. And that is how some people got into Fondoms, manipulated traditional rulers in the name of wanting to get a good catch for their party and thereby created factions. In fact, if the Fons in traditional Bamenda got into serious trouble in their constituencies, it was largely due to the fact that different political parties came lobbying the Fon and one party won, thereby transforming the Fon into a partisan institution bound to divide and destroy the very people it was meant to serve.

Another factor that greatly influenced the institution of Fon in traditional

5 Cf. Vikas Shan MBE, *Money and Human Development,* in https://thoughteconomics.com/money-and-human-development/

Bamenda was the administration of Government, which is largely an inheritance of the French colonial system. Appointed Governors, SDOs, and DOs are parachuted from "stranger" territories, some without the slightest idea of the culture of the people, to administer the people. Hence, we find a youngster who, because he holds one of these posts, imagines that he is the most important authority in the land. In fact, some even refer to themselves as *"Chef de Terre"* (owner of the land) when the people deep within know that only the Fon who pours libation and offers sacrifices for the fertility of the land, exclusively "owns the land."

Law No. 2019/024 of 24 December 2019 instituting the general code for regional and local authorities establishes a House of Chiefs for the North West and South West Regions. When placed in the context of a changing society, the Government Bill indicates a great shift from the original Southern Cameroons' House of Chiefs which the British established. Here is what the 2019 Bill says:

LAW NO 2019/024 OF 24 DECEMBER 2019

BILL TO INSTITUTE THE GENERAL CODE OF REGIONAL AND LOCAL AUTHORITIES

PART V

SPECIAL STATUS OF THE N. W. AND S. W REGIONS

CHAPTER II

ORGANS OF THE N.W AND S. W. REGIONS

Section 330: The Organs of the North West and South West Regions shall be: *the Regional Assembly* & the *Regional Executive Council.*

Section 332, *paragraph 2*: The Regional Assembly shall comprise two houses: the *House of Divisional Representatives* and the *House of Chiefs.*

1.2 HOUSE OF CHIEFS

Section 336: The *House of Chiefs* shall comprise 20 (twenty) members from among traditional rulers elected in accordance with the laws in force.

Section 337: (1) The *House of Chiefs* shall rule on all matter falling within the powers of the Regional Assembly.

(2) It shall give its opinion on the following issues:

- the status of the traditional chiefdom

- the management and conservation of historical sites, monuments and vestiges.

- the organization of cultural and traditional events in the Region.

- the collection and translation of elements of oral tradition.

Section 338: The House of Chiefs shall comprise 2 (two) committees, namely: the Committee on Administrative and Legal Affairs and Standing orders, Education, Health, Population, Social and Cultural Affairs, Youth and Sports;

the Committee on Finance, Infrastructure, Planning, Economic Development, Environment, Regional Development, State Property, Town Planning and Housing.

Section 339: (1) The *House of Chiefs* shall be chaired by the President of the Regional Executive Council, assisted by the Regional Executive Council Secretary. 2) Where the President of the *House of Chiefs* is absent or unavailable, the eldest member shall chair House proceedings. 3) Parliamentarians of the Region may take part in the proceedings of the *House of Chiefs* in advisory capacity.

Section 340: Houses of the Regional Assembly shall be convened by the President of the Regional Executive Council.

Section 341: (1) The two Houses shall meet separately on the same dates. (2) They shall hold a joint meeting a) at the opening and closing of the session, b) when the agenda item relate to the approval of the

> Regional Executive Council action programme; and the validation of the Regional Executive Council progress report at the end of the financial year. c) when circumstances so require.

This text clearly states that the House of chiefs will give only an "opinion" on the "status of the traditional chiefdom." In philosophy, an *opinion* is a view which one holds with the fear that the truth may be on the other side. Plato is the first to have thematized *opinion* in philosophy. In *The Republic*, he makes a distinction between *doxa* (an opinion) and *episteme* (knowledge). In other words, an opinion assumes the very subjective part of one's words. It is based more on a feeling than on a reality shared and observed by all.[6] Many philosophers (Aristotle, Libnitz, Kant, Hobbes etc.,) considered an "opinion" as a view built on the probable, not on facts. Such a view of the contribution of the House of Chiefs, does not seem to recognize the fundamental and divine rights of the Fons as the final authority in their Fondoms. That is why unless otherwise interpreted, this text could create a conflict with the authority of the Fon in traditional Bamenda. As a high priest of the people, the Fon has sacred and moral authority over his subjects; and this is sanctioned by the ancestors. So, the veracity of what he is says is not easily contested. In fact, people come to the Fon for knowledge (*episteme*) and wisdom (*sophia)* not for "opinion" (*doxa*).

In our political evolution, an approach where a Minister, Governor, SDO or DO has the last word even in a Fondom, we are bound to have a conflict of authority between the traditional and the modern. The modern has the force of the military to enforce its authority but deep within, the people of traditional Bamenda, are more attached to their traditional authority, the Fon. Although the armed conflict destroyed a lot, it did not succeed to erase ethnic identities; and that is the reason why, notwithstanding social change, it would be easier to reconstruct ethnic identity among the people.

b) Reconstructing Ethnicity and Identity

There are over 300 different ethnic groups in Cameroon, and each has its own identity, for which they will fight to any extent to keep. As we have said before, we live in a fast changing world and life is too complicated for any one individual to face all the challenges and difficulties. Hence, even when they find themselves out of their natural geo-ethnic habitat, people from the same

6 Cf. Tim, "Opinion: Philosophical definitions, April 17, 2017," in *Philosophy & Philosophers*, April 17, 2017, https://www.the-philosophy.com/opinion-philosophical-definitions.

group come together to build their own "symbolic environment" and "substitute world."[7] That explains why there would be a Bafut *manjong* in Washington DC; a Nso' *mfuh* in Berlin, and a Bamileke *tontin* in Ottawa, the same as you will have "meetings" of Nwa sons and daughters in Yaounde; Kom family in Douala and Aghem children in Bertoua. People want to belong and they are not ready to lose their identity. The feeling for one's ethnic group is so strong that if not well handled, it can easily lead to "tribalism" and balkanization of the society.

Hence ethnicity must always be understood in the context of human beings who want to identify with their kith and kin. Today we have more complicated issues to handle about the ethnicity and identity of some people who are children of different worlds. They concern those who we have referred to as *hybrids*. In biology, a hybrid is the offspring resulting from combining the qualities of two organisms of different breeds, varieties, species or generally through sexual reproduction. Hybrids here refer to children from parents of different cultural backgrounds; the categories are varied and enormous. A typical case today is that of a Bamileke man from Cameroon who marries a wife from among the Masai from Kenya and their children are born and bred in London. These *hyper-hybrids* seem to have little grounding in their cultural background but in an African society which is mostly patrilineal, the children will identify with the Bamilekes when they begin to seek their roots. Otherwise, they will develop a global culture of the digital natives.

A good number of the youth who were engaged in the violence which led to the denigration of the Fons in traditional Bamenda, belonged both to the military and the non-state armed militias. Many of these either came from the *hybrid* class, or those who had dropped out of school, or who did not like schooling. True education makes a human being more sensitive to the dignity and sacredness of each person, helps the educated to understand and respect the ethnicity and identity of everyone. That is why to understand the complex situation of the Fons in the aftermath of the armed conflict, it is important to point to the quality of ethnicity and identity of all the stakeholders. People who are not well grounded in their own cultural milieu and who hardly know their real identity will not respect the institution of Fon.

And that explains why many young people ransacked palaces, burned down ancestral shrines and scorched entire villages. Their value-systems were different from those of the custodians of these legacies and those who understand the deep

7 Cf. Rishikeshav Regmi, *Ethnicity and Identity*, Paper Presented in the National Seminar, Kathmandu: HMGl Nepal, Ministry of Local Government, 1995.

significance of culture as an identity of a people. It is therefore not just important to reconstruct the edifices which were destroyed, it is much more important to reconstruct ethnicity and identity, albeit taking cognizance of the fact that social constructions are shaped by and embedded in social, historical, and political contexts. The lost status and dignity of the Fon in traditional Bamenda cannot therefore be restored without a sincere reconstruction of ethnicity and identity.

In a digital era, there is always the shifting danger of more experimentation and reinvention of identity because there are equally more ways of expressing and accessing identity. People of our world very easily today can easily become who they are/were not because the power-game today is played on social media and other mobile utilities. So, many people can become too comfortable with virtual, rather than real existence.[8] This must not be allowed to happen in traditional Bamenda. People must be made to retrieve their self-worth, the dignity and sacredness of human life, and then to re-evaluate themselves: *Who are we? Where are we going to? What do we want?* Only when people begin to ask and correctly answer these questions will they be able to recognize the reality of the cultural sacrilege that was committed, and see the absolute need for restitution.

c) Repairing Cultural Sacrilege and Ancestral Anger

In traditional Bamenda, Culture is the standard for morality - this is done, that is not done! The mission of the Fon as custodian of culture is to re-enforce this morality and make sure that good is done and evil avoided. When culture is broken, the link with the Ancestors and the spirit-world is ruptured. And to repair this damage there is an elaborate but well known ritual for simple offenses and misdemeanours; but when it comes to more serious issues the ritual becomes even more complicated especially when we are dealing with a sacrilege.

The term "sacrilege" originates from the Latin *sacer*, meaning **sacred,** and *legere*, meaning *to steal.* In ancient Roman times it referred to the plundering of temples and graves. By the time of Cicero, sacrilege had adopted a more expansive meaning, including verbal offenses against religion and undignified treatment of sacred objects.

In practically every religion, sacrilegious acts are regarded with strong disapproval by the public, even by nominal or former members and non-adherents of the offended religion, especially when these acts are perceived as manifestations of hatred toward a particular sect or creed. A sacrilege is therefore a taboo.

8 Cf. John Palfrey and Urs Gasser, *Born Digital. Understanding the First Generation of Digital Natives*, Basic Books, Philadelphia, 2008, pp. 17-27.

In Catholic vocabulary, the word is used to describe any gross and deliberate profanation, blasphemy, or disrespect towards a sacred place, object or person. By derivation therefore, what some Fons did and what was done to some Fons, to palaces and shrines was tantamount in "African Traditional Religion," to a cultural sacrilege; an abomination for which there is an urgent need to make amend. The land was adulterated, atrocities were committed, and the Ancestors await appeasement or the worse yet may still happen against the community.

The community includes both the living and the "living-dead" or those who have physically died but are believed to be alive in the spirit world. Some died as good people, and others were bad; the good spirits formed the world of the deities while the bad formed the principalities. Among the deities are those who were titled elders and heads of ethnic and clan groups. These are the ones who are referred to as Ancestors, venerated and sought for, in times of difficulties and challenges. Africans believe that their ancestors are the closest people to the Most High God, therefore their intercession is always important. People who commit anti-cultural acts, annoy the ancestors who can cause evil to befall a family, or an ethnic group or clan.[9]

Ancestors are always referred to as "father" or "mother. They have the advantage that they lived with their kinsmen, so they know the difficulties in society. Since they have recently travelled the journey beyond and are now with "God the Moulder," they are in the privileged position to seek the intercession of the Almighty. Hence, they are invoked during incantations, libation, and sacrifices. Furthermore, since the ancestors had authority over the community as leaders, now that they are with the Moulder, they have greater control over earthly elements and are able to fight the bad spirits which haunt the living.[10] When the living commit acts against culture, it is believed that they anger the Ancestors who need to be appeased, so that the right harmony may continue to exist between the living and the living-dead. The ancestors must be shown respect through ritual and sacrifice.

Although rituals differ from place to place, they are similar, and often consist of pouring libation and making some incantations apologizing for the acts committed and making a promise that a repeat would be avoided. If all or some of those concerned are dead, then an animal sacrifice may be necessary to cleanse

9 Cf. Tatah Mbuy, *The Faith of our Ancestors. New Perspectives in the Study and Understanding of African Traditional Religion,* ARISE, Bamenda, 2012, pp. 85-95. Also J.S. Mbiti, *African Religions and Philosophy*, Heineman, London, 1968, pp 81-90.

10 Tatah M buy, *ibidem*, p. 56.

the land. And depending on the gravity of the fault, the animal ranges from a chicken to a goat, or cow. When it comes to a sacrifice to cleanse the land, as was the case of post conflict Bamenda, it is the sole responsibility of each Fon as the chief high priest of the clan. But, if the Fon is one of the offenders, or he is the sole offender, then the sacrifice is performed by the most important elder. In Nso' country, there is an official traditional acolyte called *Taawong* who is mandated to carry out such sacrifices in the name of the people. After the sacrifice, the blood of the animal is sprinkled both on the sacrificial stone and on the people who participated in the sacrifice. If the ancestors are satisfied, it is believed that they would show a sign to the elders.

The need to cleanse the land in traditional Bamenda has become the primary and urgent obligation given the horrors that were committed in flagrant disrespect of the people, their culture and their ancestors. And even when the ancestors have been appeased, much more is still needed to rebuild the social psyche of the people and to help them accept what happened, come to terms with it and move on with their lives.

d) Rebuilding the Social Psyche

The Social Psyche has to do with how the thoughts, feelings, and behaviours of individuals are influenced by the actual, imagined, and implied presence of others. The people of traditional Bamenda were influenced in different ways by the experiences during the armed conflict.

What happened to the Fon was both an individual and collective cultural sin, for which everyone in the group feels and takes blame. People experienced traumas and needed healing; relationships were broken and need to be repaired. Hence the need to rebuild social psyche, reformulate or orientate the thinking of people; control the influences which brought about the disorder, and re-direct the actions of everyone in society. Yet to rebuild this social thinking is neither a single entity nor a set of behaviours that one has to teach, nor a single approach to impart. Social thinking helps people on what to do when faced with a social crisis; it teaches individuals to always consider the points of view, emotions, and intentions of others. Social thinking is a language and cognitive-based methodology that focuses on social communication towards social problem solving.[11] This means that we need to teach people to understand the centrality of community, the indispensable dignity of each individual member and the

11 Pamela June Crook, et al., *Thinking socially: teaching social knowledge to foster social behavioral change. Topics in Language Disorders*, 36(3), 2016, pp. 284-298.

need for the common good. Once we get people to think in this manner, their words and actions will articulate their thinking.

During the armed conflict which negatively influenced the status of Fon in traditional Bamenda, social thinking, words and actions were either absent or misdirected against the common good. Hence, it is important to rebuild the social psyche or mind of the people by first retrieving their lost sense of *Ubuntu* (I am because we are, and because we are, therefore I am). In this way they will once again interiorize the fact that Africa and Africans are defined by their community-oriented manner of thinking and acting - the Community is the matrix of human existence in Africa.[12]

One of the values in African social thinking is the fact that no matter how angry or upset a human being is, he neither insults elders nor treat traditional authority with disdain; and on this note, what happened to the institution of Fon is a case in point. The Fon was wooed into partisan politics and by that act, the community was divided and set on edges. Furthermore, even those who considered the Fon as "auxiliaries of administration" did no more than take away the real status and dignity of the institution of Fon. So, from whichever perspective we considered the Fon, he lost and conceded more than he gained by personally being a part of competitive politics. That is why it is important that social thinking in traditional Bamenda should converge on the restoration of the former dignity of traditional rulers in general, and that of the Fon in particular.

In this chapter then, we have tried to show that there is a need to reconstruct identities if we need to restore the dignity of the Fon in traditional Bamenda. Only when each group of people begin to realize that their community has no meaning without the spiritual clan head, can we become more aware that we did ourselves evil. We committed a cultural sacrilege by defying, attacking and killing in some instances, instead of educating our Fons. The aftermath of the armed conflict has made us more aware of the horrendous crimes and atrocities that were committed and the absolute need to rebuild social thinking. Perhaps only in this way can we construct the right platform for take off to restore the dignity of the Fons in traditional Bamenda.

12 Tatah Mbuy, *Op.Cit.*, pp. 58-60.

Chapter 7

RESTORING THE DIGNITY OF THE FON

Figure 7.1. Prof. Bernard Nsokika Fonlon: Shufai Ntooh Ndzev

Traditional Bamenda is in a process of profound sociological, political, economic and cultural evolution; but if true development, unity, justice and peace are to return to this area, it is imperative to review and restore the dignity of the Fon. And to do this, we need to be concrete, practical and realistic. So, this chapter sets out four bold proposals on how this could be done.

a) Financial Autonomy to Perform a Divine Service

One of the main reasons why the institution of the Fon in traditional Bamenda went into crisis, was largely due to the fact that the Fon was almost abandoned to sort out his pertinent issues as an individual; and many of these issues needed concrete financial support. So, some of the Fons turned to where they could easily get assistance; and it was in this process that these Fons gradually traded off the original concept of their 'authority" and dignity. They pushed to the background their vocation to Divine Service and accepted instead, a new status of paid "auxiliaries of administration!" And as the English say: "he who pays the piper, calls the tune!" That is how Fons in traditional Bamenda swallowed the bait, hook, line and sinker.

Figure 7.2. Some Fons of the North West

The ideal of Fon being a chief high priest, a custodian of culture and a sacred person was not strong enough to help Fons who had concrete personal issues like the education of princes and princesses to handle. And this should not surprise us because in Maslow's hierarchy of needs, physiological needs are basic and form the foundation of the pyramid. Only those who are well-formed, motivated and have deep convictions can rise beyond physiological needs to self-actualization needs.[1] And herein lay the beginning and end of much of the problems which affected the Fons in traditional Bamenda.

In this chapter we make some concrete suggestions as to how to disentangle these difficulties which are sure to show their ugly faces again. To do this, we must first retrieve and present the original dignity and the almost exclusive mission of the Fon as chief high priest of each ethnic group.

1 Cf. Abraham Maslow, *Motivation and Personality*, Harper and Brothers, New York, 1954, pp. 35-58.

A possible obstacle for many today is the popular understanding of ***authority*** almost exclusively as an administrative and political ***power*** over others. But the Bible, one of the oldest documents in human archives, tells us that "authority" is a ***service*** to others. When St Peter wrote to the Romans, he clearly told them that "*All authority comes from God*" (Rom 13:1). Then, Jesus told his apostles that "*the Son of Man did not come to be served, but to serve, and to give his life as a ransom for many.*" (Matt. 20:28). That is why, in his first letter, St Peter advises us: "*Be shepherds of God's flock that is under your care, watching over them - not because you must, but because you are willing, as God wants you to be; not pursuing dishonest gain, but eager to serve.*" (1 Pet. 5:2). ***Authority*** properly understood is therefore for service; and the Bible is not alone in stating this!

In sociology *authority* is seen and defined in terms of a ***legitimate means*** given to an individual to bring together the different resources of the society for the "common good." That is why many sociologists make a distinction between "authority" and "power." They understand "power" as "the ability to have one's will carried out despite the resistance of others."[2] The German sociologist Max Weber, taught that while ***power*** is the ability to exercise one's will over others, ***authority*** gives one the moral obligation to work for the good of the majority and to serve them.[3] So, sociology sees "authority" as an obligation to render service by coordinating all the available talents and resources of a group towards the genuine evolution of society.

In philosophy, the notion of "authority" also involves both expertise and the right given to someone who has the qualities to coordinate the differences among the people of a society towards achieving their expected objective and final goal. Authority in philosophy definitely differs from ***power*** where obedience may even be extorted by the use of force. Hence, when moral philosophers for example, speak of ***authority,*** they actually mean the obligation to render service to one's society.[4]

Unfortunately, in modern politics, there is a very thin line between ***authority*** and ***power***, especially as politicians are more interested in having a legitimate base from which they can influence others and take decisions about the society.

2 Cf. "Power and Authority" in *Sociology,* https://open.lib.umn.edu/ sociology/chapter/14-1-power-and-authority/. Retrieved 26 March 2021.

3 Cf Max Weber, *Economy and society: An outline of interpretive sociology*, (G. Roth & C. Wittich, Eds.), University of California Press, Berkeley, 1978.

4 Cf. Green Leslie, "Authority" in *Routledge Encyclopedia of Philosophy*, Taylor and Francis, 1998.

Many politicians are Machiavellian[5] and believe that every means is permitted as long as their objective is attained. So, they may have a plan of action in their minds but once they have a legitimate base, they will do everything to ensure that their ideas are implemented, whether there is informed opposition or not.

In traditional Bamenda, although the Fon was a hereditary institution, the moral obligation to choose an heir to the throne gave the elders the opportunity to get nothing but the best from among the possibilities. In fact, the reigning Fon, before he died would have groomed one of the heirs, whose identity he only revealed to these elders on his dying-bed. This gave the *Fon-Makers* a good platform to use when the moment of choice reached. More often than not, these elders made the right choice, reason why there was often little or no opposition. The people believed that the choice was inspired by the enlightenment from the ancestors, for whom ***authority was meant for service*** to the community. And, authority seen in this light, was good and Divine deserving of obedience from everyone because each of us is a creation of God.

God created us out of love and for love; hence Divine authority is motivated by love. Love has no other preconditions except to wish the good of the other. That is why love includes service to others. God is love; and He so loved the world that He came into our history in the Person of Jesus Christ. Christ came to serve humankind and to offer his life as a ransom for all. These are Christian ideals which are also loaded in the concept and reality of the "authority of the Fon" in traditional Bamenda.

As an individual, the person who is Fon simply cannot take up any leadership role in partisan politics because, as an institution, he is a symbol of neutrality, objectivity, justice and peace. He cannot therefore function as a member of one party over another because he has authority over ***all*** his subjects who belong to different rival parties. And that is why the authority of the Fon is meant to serve all and sundry, and should at no time therefore, ever be limited to just a group of individuals.

The British quickly understood what was at stake when they had to deal with the Fons and Chiefs. That is why they decided to create the Southern Cameroons House of Chiefs as an institution which would help the British to be of better service to the people. This is how the British cherished and exploited the fact that the Fon was always considered as an impartial figure in society.[6] As long as

5 Niccolò di Bernardo dei Machiavelli (1469-1527) was an Italian diplomat, philosopher, politician, historian and writer who lived during the Renaissance. He taught that the "end justifies the means."

6 Cf. Peter Geschiere, "Chiefs and Colonial Rule in Cameroon: Inventing Chieftaincy, French

the divine authority and dignity of the Fon was maintained, the British could get the way out in their administration of the Bamenda Grassfields.

It is this same authority and dignity that must be restored today if the Government administration has to make any deep impact among the people of traditional Bamenda. And, for this to happen, traditional authority must be restored to reflect its original call to service in love and justice. In concrete terms, Government administration must respect the fact that every traditional ruler, especially the Fon, *is an institution for everyone and therefore to be excluded from partisan politics* as it operates in Cameroon. This means that every traditional ruler must not publicly be seen to be a member of this or that party. Their sentiments for one party over the other must remain a very personal affair to be discretely managed.

In fact, this should have been the attitude of every civil servant or administrator of whatever rank. *The Washington Post* of 25 October 1987, carried a very thought-provoking article on "Civil Servants in Partisan Politics?" Among many other observations, the article noted:

> The adverse consequences of permitting civil service employees to engage in partisan politics are so great as to make it unacceptable. Why? If this were to happen, citizen confidence in the impartiality of the civil service would erode rapidly. Many citizens would have strong doubts about the objectivity of those who fought them in political campaigns and who then were involved in investigations or decisions that adversely affected them - dealing with such issues as taxes, eligibility for individual and corporate benefits, compliance with regulations and procurement contracts. Public trust in the administration of government would be undermined to a dangerous degree.[7]

Mutatis mutandis, every Fon in traditional Bamenda who gets involved in partisan politics contradicts the very institution which he incarnates. Since the Government needs the Fons in the administration of the State, these rulers have a right to a state remuneration for the services they render to Cameroonian citizens in their different constituencies. But all the subjects in each Fondom equally owe an obligation to ensure the financial sustainability of their Fondom. This

---

and British Style" in *Africa*, International African Institute, Volume 63, Issue 2, April 1993, pp. 151–175.

7 Cf. *Washington Post*, "Civil Servants in Partisan Politics?" 25 October 1cf987, p. 8.

would give each Fon such financial autonomy that those of them in the House of Chiefs, or those appointed to civil service duties by virtue of competence, would be able to set the right example of what it means to be called a "Civil Servant" - one who works selflessly for the common good.

The first movement towards the restoration of the dignity of the Fon is for everyone both in Government and otherwise, to recognise that a Fon in the Bamenda Grassfields is primarily a sacred institution, a custodian of culture and the chief high priest. The Fon is the summit and incarnation of neutrality, justice and fairness. Therefore, he cannot, should not be an active element in partisan or competitive politics. All civil administrators in any Fondom in traditional Bamenda would gain more if they are conscious of the cultural structure and adherence of the people. In fact, it would be to the advantage of any civil administrator that the Fon remains a neutral party and therefore one that can easily be consulted and used for reconciliation and conflict resolution. The Fons always carried out this mission admirably until the events which have rocked society since 1990.

It is the duty of the state to remunerate anyone who helps in bringing about justice, peace and unity in the country. The Fons in traditional Bamenda were admired for the way in which they brought about peaceful coexistence and harmonious living among their subjects; and this remains a great asset to be incorporated into our modern political system.[8] Therefore, the fact that the State gives some stipend to each of the Fons and chiefs, is part of the duty of Government, not an enticement. However, all the subjects of each Fondom in Bamenda need to come together and decide on concrete ways of how to ensure the financial independence and sustainability of their Fon. In this way the Fons will be freer to act as the institutions that they were meant to be – to act for the common good.

b) Working for the Common Good

The concept and reality of the *Common Good* has become problematic in recent political and social concerns. Yet the "common good" has been, under one name or another, a recurring theme throughout the history of political philosophy.[9]

8 Cf. Michael Tabuwe Aletum, *Political conflicts within the traditional and the modern institutions: a case study of the Bafut-Cameroon*, Vander, Louvain, 1974.

9 Cf. B.J, Diggs, "The Common Good as Reason for Political Action" in *Ethics*, vol. 83, No. 4, University of Chicago, 1973.

Aristotle, for example, used the idea of "the common interest" (*to koinei sympheron)* as the basis for his distinction between "right" constitutions, which are in the common interest, and "wrong" constitutions, which are in the interest of rulers.[10] St Thomas Aquinas, the Angelic Doctor, held that "the common good" (*bonum commune)* was the goal of law and government.[11] John Locke, the 18th century English philosopher and physician, declared that "the peace, safety, and public good of the people" are the goals of political society, and further argued that "the well being of the people shall be the supreme law."[12] David Hume the Scottish thinker, contended that "social conventions" are adopted and given moral support in virtue of the fact that they serve the "public" or "common" interest.[13]

James Madison, the 4th President of the United States, wrote of the "public," "common," or "general" good as closely tied with justice and declared that justice is the end of government and civil society,[14] while Jean-Jacques Rousseau understood "the common good" (*le bien commun*) to be the object of a society's general will.[15]

Although these thinkers differed significantly in their views of what the ***common good*** consists in, as well as over what the state should do to promote it, they nonetheless agreed that the ***common good*** is the end of government, that it is the good of all the citizens, and that no government should become the "perverted servant of special interests."[16] Briefly speaking then, the ***Common Good*** refers to that which is shared and beneficial for most members of a given community.

Perhaps the most expressive form of mutual concern is the form that Plato sets out in the *Republic.*[17] Members of his ideal community conceive of themselves as working for one another's good as they play their respective roles in society as farmers, soldiers, political officials, and so on. Moreover, they not only identify with one another's good or interests, but actually *feel* one another's pleasures and pains.[18] Therefore, if we hope to retrieve the dignity of the Fon in

10 Cf. Aristotle, *Politics*, 3, 6-7, 12.

11 Cf. Thomas Aquinas, *Summa Theologiae,* 1, 2, 90, 2 and 4.

12 Cf. John Locke, *Second Treatise of Government,* Awn sham Churchill, 1969, pp. 131, 154.

13 Cf. David Hume, *Treatise on Human Nature*, Penguin, 1986.

14 Cf. James Madison, (Publius), *Federalist Papers,* New York, 1787.

15 Cf. Jean Jacques Rousseau, *Social Contract,* 1762.

16 Cf. B.J Diggs, *Ibidem.*

17 Cf. Plato, Republic, *Op.Cit.*, 462a–466d.

18 *Ibidem,* 462b–e.

traditional Bamenda, the concept and reality of the *Common Good* must come back to the centre of public affairs. Traditionally, in the Bamenda Grassfields, a Fon is synonymous to the "common good," to that institution which guarantees justice and peace.

Unfortunately, we live in a society where individualism, self-centredness, greed and selfishness, have greatly compromised the beautiful African belief in sharing whatever we have. This value has been sacrificed in our encounter with other cultures; and the result has been the continuous construction of *cultural hybrids* among whom we witness a nauseating greed that was never part of our culture. That is why it has become imperative that the *Fon-Makers* maintain today the criteria for choosing the right heir to the throne.

At the same time, once a Fon is instated, he will need to commit himself and his institution to promoting solidarity and fraternity among the people. And if any Fon is incapable of bringing this reality into existence, he will soon find out that he has become irrelevant. In fact, the Fons in traditional Bamenda who remained close to their people, even in the height of the most outrageous attacks during the five-year armed conflict, have maintained their dignity, saved their cultural patrimony, and kept the Common Good. In traditional Africa in general, and Bamenda in particular, a person's worth and value is not rated by what he has and how much "power" he wields; he is judged by how well he relates with his people and how much interest he puts in ensuring the realization of the ***Common Good***. This is what the people expect their Fons to do or forever mar their dynasty.

Already in 1990, Paul Mzeka wrote with nostalgia about the Fon who was always identified as the custodian of culture, the incarnation of the people and the defender and promoter of the common good.[19] In 2011, Prof. Chem-Langhëe and Verkijika Fanso, expressed similar feelings when discussing the institution of Fon.[20] Unalloyed concern for the ***common good*** is crucial if the dignity of the Fon has to be restored anywhere in traditional Bamenda; and this will not happen if the Fon is at the same time an active agent of partisan politics in Cameroon. This concern has become so pertinent that it has become a crucial element in the choice of a new Fon for any ethnic group.

19 Cf. Paul Mzeka, *The Four Fons of Nso', Nineteenth and Early Twentieth Century Kingship in the Western Grassfields of Cameroon*, Spider Publishing Enterprise, 1990.

20 Cf. Bongfen Chem-Langhëe and Verkijika G. Fanso (eds.), *Nso' and Its Neighbours: Readings in the Social History of the Western Grassfields of Cameroon*, Langaa RPCIG, 2011.

c) The Choice of the Best to Rule

In his *Republic*, Plato categorically stated that only the Philosopher-King should rule. By this, he actually meant that the best people should be chosen to be in authority, and the right people should also be called upon to make this choice. These two elements are part of the canons for the choice of a Fon in traditional Bamenda. Not just anyone can become Fon; nor is the Fon chosen and enthroned by just anyone.

One of the most dreadful consequences of partisan politics in contemporary Cameroon has been the deliberate attempt to politicise the institution of Fon. In fact, there have been instances where some Government Administrators (SDOs and DOs) completely ignorant of the culture and rituals involved, were found meddling in the choice and enthronement of traditional rulers in certain communities.

In traditional Bamenda, there were special Elders or *Fon-Makers* who had the sole authority to decide who will be the next Fon in a Fondom. No decree or decision from any administrator of whatever rank can truly "make a Fon" in traditional Bamenda, because this choice involves a clearly articulated ritual and well-known criteria to determine who is eligible and who is not; and from these who are *probabilias,* the council of elders, acting on the suggestion of the late Fon, can then choose the next heir. And that is why their choice is hardly contradicted or rejected. Five crucial criteria are common to all the ethnic groups when it comes to choosing who is the best heir to the throne.

First, the candidate must have the legitimate "royal blood" and *belong to the lineage that should take over*. And for this, the elders do not make a mistake because it is not possible to put on the throne one who hasn't the royal competence.

Second, the *moral character of the candidate* is very much examined. In most of Africa, the human being is defined by his character, the reason why in Nso' the people say: "*Wir dze lii*" (the human being is character). Possession and education only add to give one candidate preference over the other, but the primary insistence is on the character of the new Fon. There is no use having a Fon who may be highly educated, has the financial means and other political connections but cannot relate well with his people. That is why in Nso'land, the people say that "*wir ze wir bi' wiri*" (a person is a person because of others). Remember that we had said earlier that the primary mission of the Fon is that of being High Priest, the one who liaises the living and living-dead. Therefore, it is important that the moral and spiritual competence of the candidate is of paramount importance. Third, in many ethnic groups, candidates to the Fonship are known and many, if not all, have lived in the palace long enough to be used to palace protocol and dealings. That is why a complete stranger to the culture or a *cultural hybrid,* would be an anomaly. The Fon is custodian of culture, therefore it goes without saying that the heir to the throne should be conversant with the culture which he is called to defend and promote.

A fourth criterion for an heir to the throne is ***maturity*** and basic wisdom, which includes docility and the humility to learn from the elders and deal directly with the ancestors. In psychology, maturity is not necessarily tied to age, but does not exclude it either. However, maturity is considered as the ability to respond to the environment being aware of the correct time and location to behave and knowing when to act, according to the circumstances and the culture of the society one lives in.[21]

According to the American psychologist, Tim Elmore[22] a truly mature person possesses seven characteristics: he is able to keep long term commitments, remains unshaken by flattery and criticism, possesses a spirit of humility, takes decisions based on character not emotions, shows gratitude, knows how to privilege others instead of the self, and seeks advice before taking serious action. A mature person is ready to ask for pardon, is merciful and seeks to do the good that will benefit all. He is good at heart and does not nurse evil against others. The Fon needs this kind of maturity because he works in team with the council of elders. Finally, the ***physical fitness*** of each candidate is also important since no one wants a Fon who will always be sickly and unable to carry out most of his work. The elders usually followed up from a distance the health history of each of the possible heirs for the throne. This helped the elders to avoid the possibility of putting an invalid or sickly person on the throne. This must remain one of the measuring rods for a good Fon, even today.

d) Restoration of the Divine Authority of the Fon

As we hinted already, in many ethnic groups in Africa, the Fon is recognized as the highest traditional authority, the traditional high-priest, the one who offers sacrifices for the cleansing and fertility of the land. He stands as the mediator between the people, their Ancestors and the Spirit world. That is why the Fon belongs to two worlds, and should be seen and respected as such. Seen in this

21 Cf. David Wechsler, *"Intellectual Development and Psychological Maturity"* in *Child Development,* vol 21, No.1, March 1950, pp. 45-50.

22 Tim Elmore, *The Marks of Maturity,* https://www.psychologytoday.com /us/blog/artificial-maturity/201211. Retrieved 2 June 2021.

light, the Fons themselves and politicians in particular, will be wary in trying to woo the Fons in traditional Bamenda into partisan politics.

The authority of the Fon is *not political*, even if he rules people who are political animals. And this is not peculiar to Africa. The Jews were expecting a political Messiah when the prophets spoke about Jesus Christ, yet when Jesus came, he was quick to tell the Jewish leaders that his *"kingdom is not of this world"* (cf. Jn.18:36) but from above. Although the Fon is human, he actually belongs to the ancestral world. So, we need to see the Fon as a special divine institution with direct link to the ancestors and the world of the spirits.

In our increasingly secular world, there is a tendency to vulgarize every institution and power, but the people of Bamenda see their Fons as the liaison with the ancestors. In fact, shortly after enthronement, many Fons in traditional Bamenda were taken to the Ancestral Shrine and left there for at least one week. During this time they had no contact with any other person in the society. It was believed that they communed exclusively with the Ancestors who, in turn were expected to give them the wisdom with which they would govern the people and intercede for them.

All of this showed the sacred origin of the power and status of the Fon. Hence the Fons are said to possess mystical, life-sustaining powers, with their own well-being intimately entwined with the well-being of their people, lands, and institutions. Sacred authorities may have more than one responsibility; a Fon can be a diviner, a king may be a prophet, a seer may be a priest, and a prophet may be a seer and diviner. Each role serves a unique yet interrelated function. Diviners and healers tend to use power positively, while witches or sorcerers use power negatively.[23]

If we all understand the significance of this and the rite associated with the enthronement of the Fon, the awesome reverence given to the Fon in traditional Bamenda would make sense. The Fon has Divine Authority, and it is this authority that some of the Fons have lost, and which we need to urgently re-instate.

Furthermore, we need to understand the fact that the dignity and identity of a people in traditional Bamenda, are incarnated in the institution of the Fon. The societies in which each ethnic group lives, is a symbolic environment, a substitute world within which each of us gains identity and a sense of belonging.[24] And that

23 Cf. Jacob K. Olupona, *African Religions. A Very Short Introduction*, Oxford University Press, Oxford, p. 38.

24 Cf. Rishikeshav Regmi, *Ethnicity and Identity*, Occasional Papers, University of Kiripur, 2003. Retrieved 4 May 2021. https://www. repository.cam.ac.uk/bitstream/handle/1810/229166/

is why in traditional Bamenda, it is impossible to dissociate ethnic identity from the institutional identity of the Fon. So, even if we do not like the individual who incarnates the institution, there is no ethnic group without a Fon, and no Fon without an ethnic group because ethnicity is the expressive aspect of identity.

OPSA_08_01.pdf?sequence=2

CONCLUSION

We set out in this work to examine the fact that some Fons in traditional Bamenda got involved in partisan politics in Cameroon, and thereby brought about confusion and a denigration not only of their personal dignity and authority but also to the entire institution of Fon. In the context of the Bamenda Grassfields where the Fon is synonymous to the ethnic group and the ancestors, such an act is tantamount to a cultural sacrilege for which redress must be sought.

Too many problems and atrocities were committed especially in the lands from where the Fons ran away out of their Fondom. However, if we truly hope to find a real solution, we must begin healing from the roots - *sanatio in radice.* This entails first, a firm desire to reconstruct ethnicity and identity, then a resolute will to restore the dignity and sacredness of the Fon. To show the possibility of achieving this, we have demonstrated that the institution of Fon as understood in traditional Bamenda is incompatible with partisan politics; therefore, the Fons in the Bamenda Grassfields should keep out of competitive politics; and no politician should tempt these rulers into the kind of politics that operates among us. At the same time, the people of each ethnic group should realise that times have changed, and the sustenance of the Fon has become an issue for concrete discussion and practical decisions.

BIBLIOGRAPHY

Aquinas, Thomas. *Summa Theologiae,* Princeton University, 2015.

Aletum, Tabuwé Michael & Cyprian Fonyuy Fisiy. *Socio-political Integration and the Nso Institutions Cameroon,* Institute of Human Sciences, Yaounde, 1989.

Aristotle. *Posterior Analytics, tr. by G. R. G. Mure,* www.britannica.com /topic/ Posterior-Analytics.

Bame, Nsamenang A & Michael E. Lamb. "Socialization of Nso Children in the Bamenda Grassfields of Northwest Cameroon," in *Cross-Cultural Roots of Minority Child Development,* Patricia M. Greenfield & Rodney R. Cocking Eds. Psychology Press, New York, 2014.

Bufang, P. *Inter-Chiefdom Conflicts in the North West Province of Cameroon from 1889-1999. Colonial and Post Colonial Influences,* Unpublished M.A Thesis, University of Yaounde 1, 2000.

Bujo, B. *The Ethical Dimension of Community. The African Model and the Dialogue between North and South,* Pauline Publications, Africa, Nairobi, 1997.

Carey, James W. "Technology as a Totem for Culture." *American Journalism,* 7:4, 242-251, 1990, DOI: 10.1080/08821127.1990.10731305

Carey, James W. "A Cultural Approach to Communication." *Communication* vol 2, no.1, 1975.

Chaucer, G. *The General Prologue.* University of Oklahoma Press, 1993.

Chem-Langhëe, Bongfen. *The Origins of the Southern Cameroons House of Chiefs.* Boston University, 1983.

Chem-Langhëe, Bongfen, & Verkijika G. Fanso (editors). *Nso' and Its Neighbours: Readings in the Social History of the Western Grassfields of Cameroon,* Langaa RPCIG, 2011.

Chilver, Elisabeth and Phyllis M Kaberry. *Traditional Bamenda: the precolonial history and ethnography of the Bamenda Grassfields,* National Government Publication, Buea, 1967.

Diggs, B. J. "The Common Good as Reason for Political Action." *Ethics, vol. 83, no. 4, 1973, pp. 283–93.*

Ettangondop, M. "Federalism in a one-party state." *Cameroon: From a federal to a unitary state, 1961-1972. A critical study, edited by* Victor Ngoh, Design House,

Limbe, 2004.

Fanso, Verkijika, G. *Cameroon History for Secondary Schools and Colleges,* Team Work Press, Bamkikaiy, Kumbo, 2017

Fokwang, J. *Historical Background to the Chiefdom of Bali Nyonga,* University of Pretoria, 2003.

Fokwang, J. Fokwang, *Mediating Legitimacy: Chieftaincy and Democratisation in Two African Chiefdoms.* Langaa Research and Publishing, 2009.

Fombad & A. S Ewang. "Election Management Bodies and Peace Building in Africa. Cameroon's Move from National Election Observatory (NEO) to Elections Cameroon (ELECAM)," *Revue Africaine des Sciences Juridiques,* no. 2, Yaounde, 2008.

Fonlon, B. "Res Una Publica." *ABBIA, Special Issue, Tenth Anniversary of the United Republic of Cameroon,* Nos 38-39-40, Yaounde, 1982.

Fowler, Ian. "Kingdoms of the Cameroon Grassfields." *Reviews in Anthropology,* 40:4, 2011, pp 292-311.

Geschiere, P. "Chiefs and Colonial Rule in Cameroon: Inventing Chieftaincy, French and British Style," *Africa,* Volume 63 , Issue 2, April 1993.

Grisword, W. *Cultures and societies in a changing world,* Pine Forge, Los Angeles, 2008.

Gwanfogbe, M. B. "Resistance to European Penetration into Africa: The case of the North West Region of Cameroon." *Journal of the Cameroon Academy of Science,* vol 13, No.3, 2017.

Kiaziku, Vincente Carlos. *Culture and Inculturation. A Bantu Viewpoint,* Pauline Publications Africa, Nairobi, 2009.

Madison, J. (Publius), *Federalist Papers,* New York, 1787.

Mair, L P. "African Chiefs Today. The Lugard Memorial Lecture for 1958." *Africa: Journal of the International African Institute,* vol. 28, no. 3, 1958.

Mbuy, Tatah. *The Faith of our Ancestors. New Perspectives in the Study and Understanding of African Traditional Religion,* ARISE, Bamenda, 2012.

Mbuy, Tatah. *Understanding Witchcraft Problems in the Life of an African,* SNAAP, Enugu, 2005.

Mbiti, J. S. *African Religions and Philosophy,* Heinemann, London, 1969.

Monk N., Lindgren M, McDonald S., Pasfield-Neofitou S. *Reconstructing Identity. A Transdisciplinary Approach,* Springer Nature, Switzerland, 2017.

Mveng, Engelbert. *Indentità Africana e Cristianismo,* Società Editrice Internazionale, Torino, 1990.

Mzeka, P. *The Four Fons of Nso', Nineteenth and Early Twentieth Century Kingship in the Western Grassfields of Cameroon,* Spider Publishing Enterprise, 1990.

Ngoh, V. *The Political Evolution of Cameroon, 1884-1961,* Unpublished, University of Portland, 1979.

Ngwa, D. F. *The Fon, Chiefs and People of Bafut in Conflict, Pre-colonial Period, 1968,* Unpublished DEA in History, University of Yaounde I, 2002.

Nkwi, P. N. "Cameroon Grassfield Chiefs and Modern Politics," in *Paideuma* 25 (1979).

Olupona, Jacob K. *African Religions. A Very Short Introduction*, Oxford University Press, Oxford, 2004.

Takougang, J. "The Post-Ahidjo Era in Cameroon: Continuity and Change." *Journal of Third World Studies,* vol.10, no. 2, 1993.

INDEX

www.ingramcontent.com/pod-product-compliance
Lightning Source LLC
LaVergne TN
LVHW011029110826
845149LV00015B/3350

* 9 7 8 1 9 5 7 2 9 6 1 2 8 *